Where is the *United States*

in **Bible Prophecy?**

Michael D. Hodge

"I am a father to Israel, and EPHRAIM is my first-born. * * Declare it in the isles afar off, and say, He that scattered Israel will gather him, and keep him, as a shepherd doth his flock." Jer. 31: 9, 10.

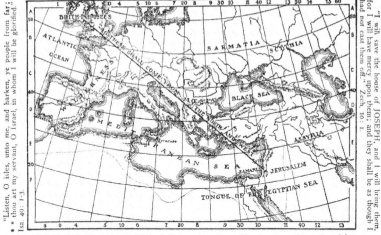

"Listen, O isles, unto me, and harken, ye people from far; * * thou art my servant, O Israel, in whom I will be glorified." Isa. 49: 1-3.

"I will save the house of JOSEPH, and I will bring them, for I will have mercy upon them: and they shall be as though I had not cast them off." Zech. 10: 1.

"Behold these (Israel in the isles) shall come from far, and lo, these from the north and from the west. The children which thou shalt have, *after thou hast lost the other*, shall say again in thine ears, The place is too strait (cramped) for me, give a place to me that I may dwell. Isa. 49: 12, 20.
EPHRAIM—ISRAEL IN THE ISLES.

Map taken from *Judah's Sceptre and Joseph's Birthright* by J. H. Allen
Used by permission Destiny Publishers Merrimac MA www.destinypublishers.com

Table of Contents

Preface

You hold in your hands a book I never expected to write. After all, others have written about this subject quite well, in fact better than perhaps I could write. After a couple of conversations I had with Jim, the Lead Pastor of my church, I was asked to have lunch with him to discuss the end times. When we met, he said to me, "Give me the unedited version of what you think." After a few minutes the subject of the identity of the United States in Bible prophecy came up and I began to explain some of what is contained in this book. At the end of that discussion, I offered to loan Jim a couple of books on the subject, one of which, though quite thorough, isn't a quick and easy read. Later, I told Jim that instead of giving him books he probably wouldn't have time to read, I'd write a summary for his further study. As I studied and started writing, I realized that what started out to be a summary would not adequately cover the subject so what you hold in your hand has turned out to be more than I expected.

I was first introduced to the subject of the connection between the United States, Britain and the Biblical *House of Israel* in 1964 while in the Air Force, away from home for the first time. I was searching for meaning to my life and God had me in Alaska where I had a lot of time to read and study the Bible. This is just one of the things God taught me at that time. During the last 45 years or so, this subject has never been far from my thinking, as God has continued to show me things, some of which have been included here. I know that sometime in the near future I need to write on some of those other subjects as well.

There are some in the church who believe we should focus solely on salvation believing that this information regarding the identity of the United States in prophecy has no relevance and, therefore the whole thing boils down to "So what?" That is a very important question and deserves a thoughtful answer which will be explored at the end of this book.

As you read the following pages, please keep your Bible handy and prayerfully consider everything. Although it has grown much longer than I expected, this book does not contain all that I have learned over the last 45 years. I encourage you to seek more on your own. There is much information available, some of which is helpful and some of which is not. God said He would send fishers and hunters for the *House of Israel* (Jeremiah 16:16).

> "Therefore behold, the days are coming," says the Lord, "that it shall no more be said, 'The Lord lives who brought up the children of Israel from the land of Egypt,' but, 'The Lord lives who brought up the children of Israel from the land of the north and from all the lands where He had driven them.' For I will bring them back into their land which I gave to their fathers. "Behold, I will send for many fishermen," says the Lord, "and they shall fish them; and afterward I will send for many hunters, and they shall hunt them from every mountain and every hill, and out of the holes of the rocks."
> Jeremiah 16:14-16

God sent fishermen immediately after the resurrection of Jesus who called His disciples "fishers of men," and He started the process of hunting them in the mid 1800s. There is a wealth of information available. You can find some resources listed in the Bibliography. A search of the internet will also provide a lot of information, of which some is helpful and some is not. In all things we must let the Holy Spirit fulfill His function to lead us into all truth (John 16:13).

Chapter 1
An Appropriate Starting Point

Introduction

The question, *"Where is the United States in Bible Prophecy?"* is one that has been asked by teachers and students of the Bible for many years. Some say one thing and some another. Many say that the most prosperous and powerful nation in the history of the world, AND the only nation founded upon Christian principles, is nowhere to be found in the Bible. I respectfully disagree with that conclusion. The problem is that most Bible students have used an invalid starting point for their search. They begin with the United States, searching for scriptures that *might* apply to her. The result is either no success, or scriptures that they think *might* refer to America. Many Bible students have been looking in the wrong place, searching for a "non-Israelite" people, a people they call "Gentiles."

Those who have been successful in finding the United States as well as Britain in Bible prophecy weren't looking for them at all, they wanted to find out whether or not the unconditional promises God made to Abraham, Isaac, Jacob, and the fathers of the twelve tribes of Israel have been fulfilled. God also made a seemingly unfulfilled but unconditional promise to king David of Israel, and this promise must also be studied. If God has not kept the promises He made to the patriarchs and to David as many believe then God and His word, and even the salvation available through His Son Jesus Christ cannot be trusted. This is a far more important question because what is at stake is the veracity of the Bible as God's word, and our ability to base our faith on more than a feeling.

The approach we will take in this study is to look at the promises, see their initial but limited fulfillment, and then face the eventual, apparent death of any hope for their completion. When we look deeper we will see how the God of resurrection took an apparently hopeless situation and fulfilled His great promises more completely than we could imagine.

God's Promises to Abram

To find the answers to the questions mentioned above, we must start in the first book of the Bible, Genesis, and with Abram, to whom God made promises and a covenant leading to the fulfilling of His plan and purpose in the earth. The history of the world for approximately the first 1900 years is covered in the first eleven chapters of Genesis, but starting in Genesis chapter 12, almost the whole rest of the Bible is the story of Abram, whose name was later changed to Abraham, and his progeny.

When God instructed Abram to leave his father's house, He made the following promise to him:

> Now the Lord had said to Abram: "Get out of your country, From your family and from your father's house, to a land that I will show you. I will make you **a great nation**; I will bless you and make your name great; and you shall be a blessing. I will bless those who bless you, and I will curse him who curses you; **and in you all the families of the earth shall be blessed**."
> Genesis 12:1-3 Emphasis added.

This is a familiar promise to most Bible students. Notice the two parts of this promise:

- A great nation
- In you all the families of the earth shall be blessed

There was a natural and national part to this promise, a promise of **race**, and there was a spiritual promise, a promise of **grace.** This same promise of grace is later repeated:

"In your seed all the nations of the earth shall be blessed."
Genesis 22:18

It is evident from the New Testament that this promise refers to Christ:

> And the Scripture, foreseeing that God would justify the Gentiles by faith, preached the gospel to Abraham beforehand, saying, "In you all the nations shall be blessed."
> Galatians 3:8

> Now to Abraham and his Seed were the promises made. He does not say, "And to seeds," as of many, but as of one, "And to your Seed," who is Christ.
> Galatians 3:16

Chapter 2
The Birthright;
The Promise of Many Nations to Abraham

God made a covenant with Abram when he was ninety nine years old. At that time He changed his name to Abraham.

> When Abram was ninety-nine years old, the Lord appeared to Abram and said to him, "I am Almighty God; walk before Me and be blameless. And I will make My covenant between Me and you, and will multiply you exceedingly." Then Abram fell on his face, and God talked with him, saying: "As for Me, behold, My covenant is with you, and you shall be a father of **many nations**. No longer shall your name be called Abram, but your name shall be Abraham; for I have made you a father of **many nations**. I will make you exceedingly fruitful; and I will make **nations** of you, and **kings** shall come from you. And I will establish My covenant between Me and you and your descendants after you in their generations, for an everlasting covenant, to be God to you and your descendants after you. Also I give to you and your descendants after you the land in which you are a stranger, all the land of Canaan, as an everlasting possession; and I will be their God."
> Genesis 17:1-8 Emphasis added.

This covenant had to do with multiple seed, a national and natural promise of offspring to a man who was childless. It was described as an everlasting covenant to be passed from generation to generation. It also included a specific land allocation for that offspring to inhabit. One of the key items that is overlooked by many is that God didn't just promise Abraham a nation, but more than one nation which would spring from him. In addition we note that these promises are to come through Abraham's wife Sarah and not through anyone else.

> And I will bless her, and give thee a son also of her: yea, I will bless her, and she shall be a mother of **nations**; kings of people shall be of her.
> Genesis 17:16 (KJV) Emphasis added.

Notice that at this time the covenant promises are conditional - "I am Almighty God; walk before Me and be blameless. And I will make My covenant between Me and you, and will multiply you exceedingly." (Verses 1-2) Later, when called upon to make the greatest sacrifice of his life, Abraham obeyed God and was willing and prepared to sacrifice his son, the only son who God had promised would carry the birthright. From this point on, the promises are unconditional.

> Then the Angel of the Lord called to Abraham a second time out of heaven, and said: "By Myself I have sworn, says the Lord, because you have done this thing, and have not withheld your son, your only son -- blessing I will bless you, and multiplying I will multiply your descendants as the stars of the heaven and as the sand which is on the seashore; and your descendants shall possess the gate of their enemies. In your seed all the nations of the earth shall be blessed, because you have obeyed My voice."
> Genesis 22:15-18

Here the promise becomes unconditional, the Lord swears by Himself. Abraham had been put to the test and passed. Notice also that there are two different kinds of offspring promised to

Abraham at this point, a natural seed comparable to the sand of the seashore, and a spiritual seed comparable to the stars of heaven (see Galatians 3:29).

The Gates of Their Enemies

Something new is also added at this point, "and your descendants shall possess the gate of their enemies." This becomes important in locating these descendants in modern times. Since God always gives Himself at least two witnesses to anything, this promise was prophesied over Rebekah by her father Bethuel and her brother Laban when she agreed to become Isaac's wife:

> And they blessed Rebekah and said to her: "Our sister, may you become the mother of thousands of ten thousands; And may your descendants possess the gates of those who hate them."
> Genesis 24:60

A gate is a narrow passage to enter or exit. When applied nationally, the term "gate" could refer to something like the Panama Canal, the Suez Canal, the Strait of Gibraltar.

The Bible must be understood on different levels. There is the natural level, much of the Bible is history and can instruct us on things that happened. There is also a spiritual level at which the Bible is to be applied. Some would want to eliminate the spiritual significance of a "gate" while others see only the spiritual application. Paul pointed out that we must first see the natural and then the spiritual.

> However, the spiritual is not first, but the natural, and afterward the spiritual.
> I Corinthians 15:46

See also I Corinthians 10:6-11 where Paul is giving an example from the Old Testament showing that we are to learn spiritual lessons from the things written so we can live godly, spiritual lives. The spiritual application of a scripture does not negate the natural application. We know that in Matthew 16:18 Jesus told His disciples that the gates of hell would not stand against the church. I believe this means both the natural and spiritual gates of hell.

A Nation and a Company of Nations

These promises were reconfirmed to Isaac and to Jacob. Ishmael and Abraham's other sons were never to be part of these promises even though Abraham told God he wished that Ishmael would live before Him and fulfill His promise.

> Then God said to Abraham, "As for Sarai your wife, you shall not call her name Sarai, but Sarah shall be her name. And I will bless her and also give you a son by her; then I will bless her, and she shall be a mother of nations; kings of peoples shall be from her." Then Abraham fell on his face and laughed, and said in his heart, "Shall a child be born to a man who is one hundred years old? And shall Sarah, who is ninety years old, bear a child?" And Abraham said to God, "Oh, that Ishmael might live before You!" Then God said: "No, Sarah your wife shall bear you a son, and you shall call his name Isaac; I will establish My covenant with him for an everlasting covenant, and with his descendants after him. And **as for Ishmael**, I have heard you. Behold, I have blessed him, and will make him fruitful, and will multiply him exceedingly. He shall beget twelve princes, and I will make him a great nation. **But My covenant I will establish with Isaac, whom Sarah shall bear to you** at this set time next year."
> Genesis 17:15-21 Emphasis added.

It was through Isaac alone that the promise was to come, so we cannot look to the Arabs, the children of Ishmael or the children born to Abraham by Keturah after the death of Sarah for the fulfillment of the promise of many nations.

Here is the confirmation of the promise to Isaac:

> There was a famine in the land, besides the first famine that was in the days of Abraham. And Isaac went to Abimelech king of the Philistines, in Gerar. Then the Lord appeared to him and said: "Do not go down to Egypt; live in the land of which I shall tell you. Dwell in this land, and I will be with you and bless you; for to you and your descendants I give all these lands, and I will perform the oath which I swore to Abraham your father. And I will make your descendants multiply as the stars of heaven; I will give to your descendants all these lands; and in your seed all the nations of the earth shall be blessed; because Abraham obeyed My voice and kept My charge, My commandments, My statutes, and My laws." Genesis 26:1-5

Notice again, this promise to Isaac is unconditional, "because Abraham obeyed My voice and kept My charge, My commandments, My statutes, and My laws."

Isaac was the father of two sons, Esau the older and Jacob the younger (See Genesis 25:19-26). God's word to Rebecca, Isaac's wife, during her pregnancy regarding these sons was that the younger would be the stronger, indicating that the younger would be preferred over the elder. Jacob eventually purchased the birthright from Esau, and received the firstborn's blessing from Isaac in which Jacob received the confirmation of the promise previously made to Abraham and Isaac.

Then his father Isaac said to him, "Come near now and kiss me, my son." And he came near and kissed him; and he smelled the smell of his clothing, and blessed him and said: "Surely, the smell of my son is like the smell of a field which the Lord has blessed. Therefore may God give you of the dew of heaven, of the fatness of the earth, And plenty of grain and wine. Let peoples serve you, And nations bow down to you. Be master over your brethren, And let your mother's sons bow down to you. Cursed be everyone who curses you, And blessed be those who bless you!"
Genesis 27:26-29

Here the promise of material wealth in the things of the ground is added with the prophecy that heathen nations would be ruled over by the birthright nations of Israel. Then in Genesis 28, there is the added dimension given that these nations of Israel would eventually spread around the world.

And behold, the Lord stood above it and said: "I am the Lord God of Abraham your father and the God of Isaac; the land on which you lie I will give to you and your descendants. Also your descendants shall be as the dust of the earth; **you shall spread abroad to the west and the east, to the north and the south;** and in you and in your seed all the families of the earth shall be blessed. Genesis 28:13-14 Emphasis added.

This spreading abroad was to be so significant that God made special allotment for the children of Israel before He established the boundaries of the rest of the nations of the world.

When the Most High divided their inheritance to the nations, when He separated the sons of Adam,

> He set the boundaries of the peoples according to
> the number of the children of Israel.
> Deuteronomy 32:8

Later, God again appeared to Jacob, changed his name to
Israel, and further defined the makeup of these "many nations"
this way:

> And God said to him, "Your name is Jacob; your
> name shall not be called Jacob anymore, but Israel
> shall be your name." So He called his name Israel.
> Also God said to him: "I am God Almighty. Be
> fruitful and multiply; **a nation and a company of
> nations** shall proceed from you, and kings shall
> come from your body.
> Genesis 35:10-11 Emphasis added.

The many nations promised to Abraham and Isaac have now
become a nation – a single great, wealthy, and powerful nation;
and another company of nations – a group, or commonwealth of
allied nations.

Chapter 3
The Scepter and the Birthright Separated

Webster's 1828 Dictionary defines Scepter:

> SCEP'TER, n. [L. sceptrum; Gr. from to send or thrust; coinciding with L. scipio, that is, a shoot or rod.] 1. A staff or batoon borne by kings on solemn occasions, as a badge of authority. Hence, 2. The appropriate ensign of royalty; an ensign of higher antiquity than the crown. Hence, 3. Royal power or authority; as, to assume the scepter.

The promise of a scepter has to do with rulership, authority and kingship.

Webster's 1828 dictionary defines Birthright:

> BIRTH'RIGHT, n. [birth and right.] Any right or privilege, to which a person is entitled by birth, such as an estate descendible by law to an heir, or civil liberty under a free constitution.
> "Esau, for a morsel, sold his birthright." Heb.12.
> It may be used in the sense of primogeniture, or the privilege of the first born, but is applicable to any right which results from descent.

Birthright is a privilege that comes to one by descent and specifically to the firstborn. This is especially true in the biblical sense. Note Webster's dictionary referring to Esau, the firstborn son of Isaac, selling his birthright to Jacob, the second-born, for some food. You can read the entire account of the birth of Isaac's twins in Genesis chapter 25. Then starting in verse 29:

Now Jacob cooked a stew; and Esau came in from the field, and he was weary. And Esau said to Jacob, "Please feed me with that same red stew, for I am weary." Therefore his name was called Edom. But Jacob said, "Sell me your birthright as of this day." And Esau said, "Look, I am about to die; so what is this birthright to me?" Then Jacob said, "Swear to me as of this day." So he swore to him, and sold his birthright to Jacob. And Jacob gave Esau bread and stew of lentils; then he ate and drank, arose, and went his way. Thus Esau despised his birthright.
Genesis 25:29-34

Jacob knew the importance of the birthright. It isn't just a spiritual inheritance to be obtained only after one dies, but it is also something that pertains to this earthly life.

During the days of Jacob/Israel the birthright and the scepter parts of the covenant promises were divided between two of Jacob's children. We'll look at where this happened shortly.

The scepter shall not depart from Judah, Nor a lawgiver from between his feet, Until Shiloh comes; And to Him shall be the obedience of the people.
Genesis 49:10

Now the sons of Reuben the firstborn of Israel – he was indeed the firstborn, but because he defiled his father's bed, his birthright was given to the sons of Joseph, the son of Israel, so that the genealogy is not listed according to the birthright; yet Judah prevailed over his brothers, and from him came a ruler, although the birthright was Joseph's–
I Chronicles 5:1-2

The birthright belongs to Joseph, but the Scepter promises apply to the tribe of Judah. This includes the promise of salvation as Jesus Himself said in John 4:22, "Salvation is of the Jews."

Part 1 - The Birthright
Jacob/Israel adopts Joseph's sons

The 48th chapter of Genesis is very important in the history of the birthright. After Jacob/Israel and his sons moved to Egypt, the time came for Israel to die, so Joseph brought his two sons to his father for a blessing. He knew that there is significance in the blessing of a father on his children, a fact that is overlooked by most people today.

The passage in Genesis 48 is too long to include here, so I will point out the significant portions.

> And Joseph took them both, Ephraim with his right hand toward Israel's left hand, and Manasseh with his left hand toward Israel's right hand, and brought them near him. Then Israel stretched out his right hand and laid it on Ephraim's head, who was the younger, and his left hand on Manasseh's head, guiding his hands knowingly, for Manasseh was the firstborn.
> Genesis 48:13-14

In this instance we see that Joseph wanted Israel's right hand on the head of the elder son because it represented the greater blessing. However, Israel placed his right hand on the younger son, thus elevating his position.

> And he blessed Joseph, and said: "God, before whom my fathers Abraham and Isaac walked, The God who has fed me all my life long to this day, the Angel who has redeemed me from all evil, Bless the lads; **Let my name be named upon them**, and the name of my fathers Abraham and

Isaac; and let them grow into a multitude in the midst of the earth."
Genesis 48:15-16 Emphasis added.

This promise of national greatness is being transferred, not to Reuben the firstborn, but to the children of Joseph. Also notice that Israel says, "Let my name be named on them, and the name of my fathers Abraham and Isaac." Also notice Genesis 48:5 where Jacob/Israel tells Joseph, "And now your two sons, Ephraim and Manasseh, who were born to you in the land of Egypt before I came to you in Egypt, are mine; as Reuben and Simeon, they shall be mine." By these statements, Israel adopted these sons of Joseph and his Egyptian wife. The name Israel now rightly belongs to them specifically and primarily. As we look later in scripture, we see the name Ephraim and Israel, House of Ephraim and *House of Israel* used interchangeably.

> Now when Joseph saw that his father laid his right hand on the head of Ephraim, it displeased him; so he took hold of his father's hand to remove it from Ephraim's head to Manasseh's head. And Joseph said to his father, "Not so, my father, for this one is the firstborn; put your right hand on his head." But his father refused and said, "I know, my son, I know. He also shall become a people, and he also shall be great; but truly his younger brother shall be greater than he, and his descendants shall become a multitude of nations." So he blessed them that day, saying, "By you Israel will bless, saying, 'May God make you as Ephraim and as Manasseh!'" And thus he set Ephraim before Manasseh.
> Genesis 48:17-20

When Joseph saw that the greater blessing was about to go to the younger son, he tried to get Israel to change, but Israel said he knew what he was doing. Notice also that now the promise of a great nation and a company of nations belong, not to the other eleven tribes, but to Joseph and specifically to his sons, Ephraim and Manasseh, who have become the holders of the birthright.

Part 2 - The Scepter

After Israel adopted and blessed the sons of Joseph in Genesis chapter 48, he called together all of his sons.

> And Jacob called his sons and said, "Gather together, that I may tell you what shall befall you in **the last days**:"
> Genesis 49:1 Emphasis added.

Jacob prophesied over all of his children in Genesis chapter 49, telling them what would happen "in the last days," in our time. According to the New Testament, we have been in the "last days" since the time of Jesus and the apostles. Among other things Jacob had this to say about Judah:

> The scepter shall not depart from Judah, Nor a lawgiver from between his feet, Until Shiloh comes; And to Him shall be the obedience of the people.
> Genesis 49:10

As we'll see shortly, it took several generations for a lawgiver to come out of Judah. The prophecy regarding Shiloh is obviously a reference to Christ who shall eternally rule upon this throne.

> Now the sons of Reuben the firstborn of Israel –
> he was indeed the firstborn, but because he defiled
> his father's bed, his birthright was given to the
> sons of Joseph, the son of Israel, so that the
> genealogy is not listed according to the birthright;
> yet Judah prevailed over his brothers, and from

> him came a ruler, although the birthright was
> Joseph's–
> I Chronicles 5:1-2

We quoted this scripture earlier, but this time notice the scripture above says that a ruler *came*, not that He would come in the future. The chronicler was speaking in the past tense from his time frame of reference. While there is certainly the Messianic aspect of the Scepter promise, there was a natural kingly line that was required to exist in order for the Messiah to come. Notice that when he comes, he will sit on a throne and govern. There was no throne of David in Jerusalem when Jesus came the first time. The Jews were ruled by Roman governors until the nation was a second time removed from Jerusalem and Judea in 70 AD. Jesus did not ascend to the throne of David, in fact He avoided being made king during his earthly life, but He must sit on that throne at some date in the future. Perhaps I get ahead of myself.

There is no doubt that God promised a king to the people of Israel and that this king would be from the tribe of Judah. I used to wonder, if that is true, and it is, then why was the first king in Israel from the tribe of Benjamin. I believe God gave me the answer to that question.

When the people asked for a king in I Samuel chapter eight, the idea didn't take God by surprise. He'd promised kings to Abraham, Isaac, and to Jacob. During the days of Moses He gave instruction regarding the choice of a king and how the king should govern.

> "When you come to the land which the Lord your
> God is giving you, and possess it and dwell in it,
> and say, 'I will set a king over me like all the
> nations that are around me,' you shall surely set a
> king over you whom the Lord your God chooses;
> one from among your brethren you shall set as
> king over you; you may not set a foreigner over
> you, who is not your brother.

Deuteronomy 17:14-15

"Also it shall be, when he sits on the throne of his kingdom, that **he shall write for himself** a copy of this law in a book, from the one before the priests, the Levites."
Deuteronomy 17:18 Emphasis added.

Notice that He didn't say "if," but "when" the people would want a king. The king was instructed to write his own copy of the law so he would know how to govern according to God's will and law.

When the people got tired of their form of government in the days of Samuel and demanded a king, God gave them Saul from the tribe of Benjamin (See I Samuel 9:1-2). After Saul proved to be disobedient to the Lord in I Samuel 15, God told Samuel to look to the sons of Jesse to find a new king. He found David and anointed him to be the next king of Israel. (See I Samuel 16:1-13)

There are some interesting things to note about the genealogy of David, but first we need to look at one of the stories we usually overlook or just say, "that is interesting." God had these stories included in His sacred word for our instruction. The story is found in Genesis 38 and it involves Jacob's son Judah, and Tamar his widowed daughter-in-law who had been married to Judah's sons Er and Onan both of whom died. You can read the story for yourself, but the significant point to this story is that Judah never married Tamar so Perez and Zerah, the twin sons she bore to him, were illegitimate. There is a little-known law in the book of Deuteronomy that applies to this issue:

One of illegitimate birth shall not enter the assembly of the Lord; even to the tenth generation none of his descendants shall enter the assembly of the Lord.
Deuteronomy 23:2

Now notice the genealogy of David as given at the end of the book of Ruth:

> And they called his name Obed. He is the father of Jesse, the father of David. Now this is the genealogy of Perez: Perez begot Hezron; Hezron begot Ram, and Ram begot Amminadab; Amminadab begot Nahshon, and Nahshon begot Salmon; Salmon begot Boaz,and Boaz begot Obed; Obed begot Jesse, and Jesse begot David.
> Ruth 4:17-22

If you start counting with the illegitimate son of Judah, Perez as #1, Hezron is #2, Ram is #3, Amminadab is #4, Nahshon is #5, Salmon is #6, Boaz is #7, Obed is #8, Jesse is #9, and David is #10; the law is fulfilled and a king can come from the tribe of Judah.

Since I am on a side journey, another question I had until recently was, why did God choose someone from Benjamin and not one of the other tribes to be the first king. And going along with that, why was the tribe of Benjamin, always connected with Judah? I believe the answer is found in another story from the life of Joseph and his brothers.

The sons of Israel, the brothers of Joseph sold him into slavery because of jealousy regarding the fact that their father showed preference to Joseph because he was the first born son of his favorite wife, Rachel, and because of the prophetic dreams he had told them about. Reuben overheard the rest of his brothers talking about killing Joseph, and talked them into putting him into a pit so he could later return and retrieve him, thus sparing his life (see Genesis 37:18-22). While Reuben was gone, the brothers saw some Ishmaelites on their way to Egypt to sell their wares.

> So Judah said to his brothers, "What profit is there if we kill our brother and conceal his blood? Come and let us sell him to the Ishmaelites, and

let not our hand be upon him, for he is our brother and our flesh." And his brothers listened.
Genesis 37:26-27

To make a long story short, once Joseph was sold, he ended up in Egypt ruling as prime minister under Pharaoh, managing the provision that had been made for the seven year famine. The first time Israel sent his sons to Egypt during the famine to obtain grain, they didn't take Benjamin because he was the youngest and the second and last son of Israel's favorite wife, Rachel, and younger brother of Joseph. Joseph told his brothers not to return unless they brought Benjamin with them.

After the famine increased, Israel again had to send his sons to Egypt to buy grain, but he didn't want to let Benjamin go because he was afraid something would happen to him and he would lose him as he'd lost Joseph. Judah saw what his earlier actions in getting Joseph sold into slavery had done to his father.

> Then Judah said to Israel his father, "Send the lad with me, and we will arise and go, that we may live and not die, both we and you and also our little ones. **I myself will be surety for him**; from my hand you shall require him. If I do not bring him back to you and set him before you, then let me bear the blame forever."
> Genesis 43:8-9 Emphasis added.

I believe the destinies of these two brothers and the tribes that sprang from them were intertwined from that time forward. Judah was always looking out for Benjamin and a special bond developed that remains to this day. As we shall see, when there was a split between the tribes of Israel you always see Judah and Benjamin spoken of as the "*House of Judah*" while the other ten tribes are called the "*House of Israel*."

If the first king of Israel could not come from the *tribe* of Judah because the ten generations had not yet been fulfilled, he could still, at least, come from the *"House of Judah."*

Abraham's Family Tree

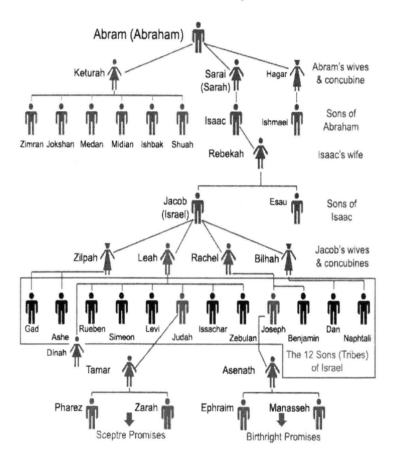

Taken from *"The U.S.A. & The British Commonwealth in Bible Prophecy"* by Peter Salemi.
Used by permission. www.british-israel.ca

Chapter 4
David's Throne and Covenant

> David was thirty years old when he began to reign, and he reigned forty years. In Hebron he reigned over Judah seven years and six months, and in Jerusalem he reigned thirty-three years over all Israel and Judah.
>
> II Samuel 5:4-5

When David took the throne following the death of Saul, he ruled for forty years; seven and a half years he ruled over the *House of Judah* only as the *House of Israel* appointed a successor to Saul's dynasty as king. Then David was accepted as king of the united nation for thirty-three years.

During David's reign God made a little known covenant with him. David wanted to build a house for God, the temple which was eventually built by David's son and successor, Solomon. Nathan the prophet told David that he would not be able to build the house because David was a man of war, but God made the following covenant with David through Nathan:

> "When your days are fulfilled and you rest with your fathers, I will set up your seed after you, who will come from your body, and I will establish his kingdom. He shall build a house for My name, and **I will establish the throne of his kingdom forever**. I will be his Father, and he shall be My son. If he commits iniquity, I will chasten him with the rod of men and with the blows of the sons of men. But My mercy shall not depart from him, as I took it from Saul, whom I removed from before you. And **your house and your kingdom shall be established forever before you. Your throne shall be established forever**."

II Samuel 7:12-16 Emphasis added.

The promise God made is not dependent upon the righteousness of David's descendants which is evidenced by verses 14 and 15 "If he commits iniquity, I will chasten him with the rod of men and with the blows of the sons of men. But My mercy shall not depart from him, as I took it from Saul, whom I removed from before you." Saul's dynasty ended, but God says that David's line will continue forever. This promise is repeated in Psalm 89:

> "I have made a covenant with My chosen, I have sworn to My servant David: 'Your seed I will establish forever, And build up your throne to all generations.'"
> Psalm 89:3-4

This covenant is described in detail later in the psalm:

> "My mercy I will keep for him forever, And My covenant shall stand firm with him. His seed also I will make to endure forever, and his throne as the days of heaven. "If his sons forsake My law and do not walk in My judgments, if they break My statutes and do not keep My commandments, then I will punish their transgression with the rod, and their iniquity with stripes. Nevertheless My lovingkindness I will not utterly take from him, nor allow My faithfulness to fail. My covenant I will not break, nor alter the word that has gone out of My lips. Once I have sworn by My holiness; I will not lie to David: his seed shall endure forever, and his throne as the sun before Me; it shall be established forever like the moon, even like the faithful witness in the sky."
> Psalm 89:28-37

This promise of a descendant to continually sit upon the throne is now said to be like the sun and the moon which are ordained to be in existence as long as this earth exists in its present form.

> "For thus says the Lord: 'David shall never lack a man to sit on the throne of the **House of Israel**;'".... And the word of the Lord came to Jeremiah, saying, "Thus says the Lord: 'If you can break My covenant with the day and My covenant with the night, so that there will not be day and night in their season, then My covenant may also be broken with David My servant, so that he shall not have a son to reign on his throne.'"
> Jeremiah 33:17, 19-21 Emphasis added.

This reference in Jeremiah is significant considering his commission to the then existing kingdom in the *House of Judah*, which we will discuss later. As far as is commonly known the last king of David's dynasty to sit upon his throne was King Zedekiah of Judah who was carried away to Babylon in 585 B.C. If the throne ceased to exist with Zedekiah, then it cannot exist today, and if that is the case, how shall Jesus sit upon a non-existent throne?

> And behold, you will conceive in your womb and bring forth a Son, and shall call His name Jesus. He will be great, and will be called the Son of the Highest; and the Lord God will give Him the throne of His father David.
> Luke 1:31-32

As mentioned before, some say that Christ took the throne of Israel when he came the first time, but He did not. It is evident from the Gospels that whenever people wanted to make Him king, he fled the scene.

Therefore when Jesus perceived that they were about to come and take Him by force to make Him king, He departed again to the mountain by Himself alone.

John 6:15

But didn't Jesus take up the kingdom when He went to heaven? Remember, we are speaking of a physical kingdom in a physical nation on the earth. God's purpose for Israel on the earth cannot be fulfilled in heaven. Again we turn to Jeremiah's prophecy regarding this throne:

> Have you not considered what these people have spoken, saying, "The two families which the Lord has chosen, He has also cast them off'? Thus they have despised My people, as if they should no more be a nation before them. Thus says the Lord: 'If My covenant is not with day and night, and if I have not appointed the ordinances of heaven and earth, then I will cast away the descendants of Jacob and David My servant, so that I will not take any of his descendants to be rulers over the descendants of Abraham, Isaac, and Jacob. For I will cause their captives to return, and will have mercy on them.'"
> Jeremiah 33:24-26

God tells Jeremiah that unless you can stop the earth from rotating on its axis, unless you can take the sun, moon and stars from the heaven, you cannot prevent Him from keeping His covenant with David to maintain his descendant on the throne ruling over at least a portion of the descendants of Abraham, Isaac, and Israel. David's dynasty was to remain in force and effect in the *"House of Israel"* as Jeremiah tells us (Jeremiah 33:17 quoted above). During the days of Jeremiah, the throne was transferred from the *House of Judah* to the *House of Israel*. But, again, I get ahead of myself.

Chapter 5
Israel Becomes Two Nations

When King David died, his son Solomon took the throne of the united kingdom of Israel. Solomon fulfilled his obligation to build the temple for God in Jerusalem for which his father David had made preparation. Afterward, Solomon began to go astray. In order to build his kingdom, his royal palace, and to maintain his excessive lifestyle, he imposed heavy taxes on the people as well as conscripting them into forced service. Solomon also married Gentile wives and sacrificed to their idols and committed other sins.

> Therefore the Lord said to Solomon, "Because you have done this, and have not kept My covenant and My statutes, which I have commanded you, I will surely **tear the kingdom away from you** and give it to your servant. Nevertheless I will not do it in your days, for the sake of your father David; I will tear it out of the hand of your son. However I will not tear away the whole kingdom; **I will give one tribe to your son for the sake of my servant David**, and for the sake of Jerusalem which I have chosen."
> I Kings 11:11-13 Emphasis added.

The kingdom, not just part of it, was torn from the dynasty of David. The part, one tribe, was to remain with David's dynasty. And the reason? "For the sake of my servant David." It was not because of Solomon, but God would not break His covenant with David. He left one tribe to be ruled by David 's dynasty.

When Solomon died, his son Rehoboam took David's throne in Jerusalem. God had already chosen Jeroboam, one of Solomon's servants to be king of Israel, so he became the spokesman for the northern ten tribes and the people demanded the heavy taxes be reduced.

> "Your father made our yoke heavy; now therefore, lighten the burdensome service of your father, and his heavy yoke which he put on us, and we will serve you."
> I Kings 12:4

Rehoboam's reply came back,

> "And now, whereas my father put a heavy yoke on you, I will add to your yoke; my father chastised you with whips, but I will chastise you with scourges!"
> 1 Kings 12:11

Israel rebelled, saying:

> "What share have we in David? We have no inheritance in the son of Jesse. To your tents, O Israel! Now, see to your own house, O David!"
> 1 Kings 12:16

So Israel has been in rebellion against the house of David to this day. Now it came to pass when all Israel heard that Jeroboam had come back, they sent for him and called him to the congregation, and made him king over all Israel. There was none who followed the house of David, but the tribe of Judah only. And when Rehoboam came to Jerusalem, he assembled all the *House of Judah* **with the tribe of Benjamin**, one hundred and eighty thousand chosen men who were warriors, to fight against the *House of Israel*, that he might

restore the kingdom to Rehoboam the son of
Solomon.
I Kings 12:19-21 Emphasis added.

Israel made Jeroboam, from the tribe of Ephraim, king of
Israel, but Rehoboam took the *House of Judah* along with the
tribe of Benjamin in order to fight to maintain control. But God
said,

> "You shall not go up nor fight against your
> brethren the children of Israel. Let every man
> return to his house, for this thing is from Me."
> I Kings 12:24

The *House of Judah*, now consisting of the tribes of Judah and
Benjamin under Rehoboam of the dynasty of David, was about to
go to war against the *House of Israel* consisting of the other ten
tribes headed by Ephraim and Manasseh. Later on, the first place
the word "Jew" is used in the King James Version and the
American Standard Version is II Kings 16:6 where we find Israel
at war with the Jews. See the entire 16th chapter of II Kings for
this complete story. The term Jews, from a Biblical frame of
reference, was never applied to the entire twelve tribes, but to the
House of Judah which includes Benjamin and much of Levi.
Also, no place in the Bible does the term "Israel" refer to the Jews
only. Technically, Abraham, Isaac, Jacob and ten of the twelve
sons of Israel were never Jews. Again, technically, the first Jew
was Israel's son Judah, from whom the Jews get their name.
Some Israelites are Jews, just as some Americans are
Missourians, but not all Israelites are Jews, just as not all
Americans are Missourians.

Now, for the first time, the birthright goes to one nation, the
House of Israel headed by Ephraim and Manasseh, while the
sceptre is entrusted to another nation, called the *House of Judah*.
The two parts of the promises to Abraham, Isaac, and Jacob are
now divided between two nations.

The promise to Jeroboam that he should become king of Israel is recorded in I Kings 11:31-39. At the end of this prophecy we read:

> "Then it shall be, if you heed all that I command you, walk in My ways, and do what is right in My sight, to keep My statutes and My commandments, as My servant David did, then I will be with you and build for you an enduring house, as I built for David, and will give Israel to you."
>
> I Kings 11:38

God told Jeroboam that he would make a covenant of dynasty with him just as he had with David on the condition that he obey God and walk in His ways. Unfortunately, Jeroboam was not a man of faith and he turned the ten tribe nation away from God almost immediately.

> And Jeroboam said in his heart, "Now the kingdom may return to the house of David: If these people go up to offer sacrifices in the house of the Lord at Jerusalem, then the heart of this people will turn back to their lord, Rehoboam king of Judah, and they will kill me and go back to Rehoboam king of Judah." Therefore the king asked advice, made two calves of gold, and said to the people, "It is too much for you to go up to Jerusalem. Here are your gods, O Israel, which brought you up from the land of Egypt!" And he set up one in Bethel, and the other he put in Dan.
>
> 1 Kings 12:26-29

By not taking God at His word, he entered into fear, and took Israel into idolatry, and the forsaking of God's law. This fear manifested itself in the fact that Jeroboam changed the Feasts of

God, moving the times of the feasts by a month so the people would not go to Jerusalem to keep God's appointed times. He also set up two golden calves to be worshiped. The result was that Israel had one king after another, nine different dynasties and nineteen kings, some evil, and some extremely evil. Jeroboam's dynasty ended with himself. However, the Jewish dynasty of David continued intact until the days of Zedekiah when the Jews were carried off to Babylon. Four whole books of the Bible, I and II Kings and I and II Chronicles, are dedicated to the history of these two separate nations and to the histories of their kings. Finally, the sins of the *House of Israel* became so great in God's sight that He caused them to be a conquered, captive nation.

In the years 721 - 718 B.C. Israel was conquered and its people were driven out of their land by Assyria. They were carried away from their own land and lost from view.

> Therefore the Lord was very angry with Israel, and removed them from His sight; there was none left but the tribe of Judah alone.
> II Kings 17:18

The northern ten tribe nation called Israel was carried away. They became known as the Lost Ten Tribes and are commonly called that today. However, the *House of Judah* remained in their land until the time of the prophet Jeremiah. Finally, Jerusalem was invaded by Nebuchadnezzar in 585 B.C. and as far as is known the last king to sit on the throne of David was Zedekiah. His sons were slain before his eyes and then he was blinded and taken to Babylon where he lived the rest of his life.

> The Chaldean army pursued them and overtook Zedekiah in the plains of Jericho. And when they had captured him, they brought him up to Nebuchadnezzar king of Babylon, to Riblah in the land of Hamath, where he pronounced judgment on him. Then the king of Babylon **killed the sons**

of Zedekiah before his eyes in Riblah; the king of Babylon also **killed all the nobles of Judah.** Moreover he put out Zedekiah's eyes, and bound him with bronze fetters to carry him off to Babylon. And the Chaldeans burned the king's house and the houses of the people with fire, and broke down the walls of Jerusalem.

Jeremiah 39:5-8 Emphasis added.

The question then becomes, did the dynasty of David really end with Zedekiah and did God break His unconditional covenant with David? If so, we cannot count on God for anything.

Chapter 6
What About Jeconiah?

In 585 B.C. when Zedekiah and the city of Jerusalem were taken into captivity a former king of Judah, Jeconiah the nephew of Zedekiah, who was in the dungeons of Babylon had sons who could continue David's line. In 604 B.C. Jeconiah, also called Jehoiachin and Coniah, was taken to Babylon in chains, but was given a place of honor some thirty seven years after becoming a captive. He was even given a title of "king" with many other captive "kings."

> Now it came to pass in the thirty-seventh year of the captivity of Jehoiachin king of Judah, in the twelfth month, on the twenty-seventh day of the month, that Evil-Merodach king of Babylon, in the year that he began to reign, released Jehoiachin king of Judah from prison. He spoke kindly to him, and gave him a more prominent seat than those of the kings who were with him in Babylon. So Jehoiachin changed from his prison garments, and he ate bread regularly before the king all the days of his life. And as for his provisions, there was a regular ration given him by the king, a portion for each day, all the days of his life.
>
> II Kings 25:27-30

Shalthiel, one of Jeconiah's sons was the father of Zerubbabel, the son of royal seed through whom the genealogy of Jesus Christ was traced back to David! (See Matthew 1:12) Zerubbabel was the man God caused Cyrus, king of Persia, to make the *governor*, not king, upon his return to Jerusalem to rebuild the House of God, the Temple, seventy years after the captivity in fulfillment of Jeremiah's prophecy of the seventy years captivity and Isaiah's prophecy (see Jeremiah 25:11-12 and 29:10 and Isaiah 44:28-45:1).

Yet neither Jeconiah nor any of his sons or grandsons reigned as king in Jerusalem. If a descendant of David's line lived through the captivity, why wasn't he restored to the throne when he returned to Jerusalem? Simply because God would not allow it to happen! God sets up kings and removes them. God had determined to remove the crown of David from the then ruling line of Perez and give it to a son of Zerah. Yet a royal remnant directly from the line of David had to remain in the area so Jesus Christ could be born of David's seed hundreds of years later. God also had to keep His promise to David that he would never lack a descendant to sit on his throne.

> "As I live," says the Lord, "though Coniah the son
> of Jehoiakim, king of Judah, were the signet on
> My right hand, yet I would pluck you off"
> Jeremiah 22:24

God was ending this line of kings, removing the *crown*, not permitting any of Jeconiah's descendants to reign on the throne of Judah. God was overturning the throne to another branch of Judah's family. God told Jeremiah:

> Thus says the Lord: "Write this man down as
> childless, a man who shall not prosper in his days;
> for none of his descendants shall prosper, sitting
> on the throne of David, and ruling anymore in
> Judah."
> Jeremiah 22:30

Although it is recorded that Jeconiah had children (see I Chronicles 3:17 and Matthew 1:12), as far as the throne of David was concerned, he was childless, none of his children ever sat on that throne.

Again, we see how God is in charge of things when it comes to fulfilling His promises and His purposes in the earth. While the kingdom, the crown, and the throne were removed from the *House of Judah*, the promise of the savior coming from the line of David and from the tribe of Judah was also fulfilled.

Now we'll look at how God, in spite of appearances to the contrary, began to fulfill His promise that a descendant of David would always sit on a throne ruling the *House of Israel.*

Chapter 7
Jeremiah's Divine Commission

> Then the Lord put forth His hand and touched my
> mouth, and the Lord said to me: "Behold, I have
> put My words in your mouth. See, I have this day
> set you over the nations and over the kingdoms,
> To root out and to pull down, To destroy and to
> throw down, To build and to plant."
> Jeremiah 1:9-10

Jeremiah's calling and commission is given in the above scripture. God Himself set Jeremiah "over the nations and over the kingdoms." Notice, more than one nation, and more than one kingdom. Sometimes we think this is just figurative and that it is not to be taken literally. Note also that his commission was to do either three or six things, depending on how you interpret verse 10.

- To root out and to pull down
- To destroy and to throw down
- To build and to plant

Jeremiah's prophetic ministry spanned from 626 B.C. to 585 B.C., a period of approximately forty one to forty two years and he prophesied to four kings of Judah, Josiah, Jehoiakim, Jehoiachin, and Zedekiah. He was approximately seventeen years old when God called him so he may have been about fifty eight to sixty years old at the end of the book that carries his name. During that time, Jeremiah fulfilled the first part of his commission, "to root out and to pull down, to destroy and to throw down." This has specific reference to the nation of Judah, to the city of Jerusalem, and to the dynasty of David in Jerusalem ruling over the *House of Judah*. But what of his calling "to build and to plant?" What was he to build, and what was he to plant?

And, where was he to build and plant? When the Jews came back to rebuild Jerusalem, where was Jeremiah? Remember, he himself prophesied that the Jews would spend seventy years in captivity and then at least some of them would return to rebuild the city in preparation for the coming of Messiah. Jeremiah would have been around one hundred and thirty years old, and there is no record of Jeremiah at that time. So what happened to Jeremiah, and did he die not having fulfilled his full commission?

As previously mentioned, the last king of Judah was Zedekiah who was taken to Babylon after his sons were killed before his eyes just before he was blinded. In addition, "all the nobles of Judah" were also killed. There was no one from the line of David left who could rule. The integrity of God's promise to David is now in jeopardy. From that time until now, there has apparently not been a king ruling over national Israel for the *House of Israel* was taken away in 721 B.C. and Zedekiah was the last king of the David dynasty to rule over the *House of Judah* when he and the city of Jerusalem were taken captive in 585 B.C. I think it is significant that, at the very time Jeremiah is prophesying the destruction of Jerusalem which brought about the apparent end of David's dynasty, he is given this very strong pronouncement from God:

> "Thus says the Lord: 'If My covenant is not with day and night, and if I have not appointed the ordinances of heaven and earth, then I will cast away the descendants of Jacob and David My servant, so that I will not take any of his descendants to be rulers over the descendants of Abraham, Isaac, and Jacob.'"
> Jeremiah 33:25-26

Again God proclaims that if we can stop the earth from turning, etc. then we can stop Him from fulfilling His promises and covenant with David that he will always have a descendant to rule over the descendants of Abraham, Isaac, and Jacob.

Remember that Israel said "Let my name be named on" Ephraim and Manasseh, the sons of Joseph.

It is not possible to recount the entire life of Jeremiah here. You can read Jeremiah's writings and the historical books of the Bible to get the whole story. What is important for our discussion is the end of the story. After the fall of Jerusalem and the captivity of the people, Jeremiah was among the captives. He needed to be free to complete the final part of his commission.

> And the captain of the guard took Jeremiah and said to him: "The Lord your God has pronounced this doom on this place. Now the Lord has brought it, and has done just as He said. Because you people have sinned against the Lord, and not obeyed His voice, therefore this thing has come upon you. And now look, **I free you this day** from the chains that were on your hand. If it seems good to you to come with me to Babylon, come, and I will look after you. But if it seems wrong for you to come with me to Babylon, remain here. See, all the land is before you; wherever it seems good and convenient for you to go, go there." Now while Jeremiah had not yet gone back, Nebuzaradan said, "Go back to Gedaliah the son of Ahikam, the son of Shaphan, whom the king of Babylon has made governor over the cities of Judah, and dwell with him among the people. Or go wherever it seems convenient for you to go." So the captain of the guard gave him rations and a gift and let him go. Jeremiah 40:2-5 Emphasis added.

Jeremiah was free to go and do as he pleased and to fulfill the last part of his commission about building and planting. Jeremiah went to Gedeliah in Mizpah to live among the people who were left in Judea (Jer. 40:6). Gedeliah was Nebuchadnezzar's appointment as governor over the remnant of Jews and he set up his government in Mizpah. When the king of Ammon plotted with a Jew named Ishmael and succeeded in killing Gedeliah and part of the Jews, Jeremiah was one of the survivors.

> Then Ishmael carried away captive all the rest of the people who were in Mizpah, **the king's daughters** and all the people who remained in Mizpah, whom Nebuzaradan the captain of the guard had committed to Gedaliah the son of Ahikam. And Ishmael the son of Nethaniah carried them away captive and departed to go over to the Ammonites.
> Jeremiah 41:10 Emphasis added.

Among the survivors with Jeremiah were **the daughters of Judah's king Zedekiah**, who were of the royal dynasty of David. Apparently Jeremiah went to Mizpah to retrieve these daughters.

> Zedekiah was twenty-one years old when he became king, and he reigned eleven years in Jerusalem. His mother's name was Hamutal the daughter of Jeremiah of Libnah.
> 2 Kings 24:18

Libnah was a Levite city given to the children of Aaron. It seems likely that Jeremiah, a priest of the tribe of Levi (Jeremiah 1:1), may have been related to these daughters of the king since he was probably Zedekiah's grandfather. If this is the case, then he would have had reason to take charge of his great-granddaughters. In either case, the king's daughters were with Jeremiah.

Ishmael was shortly replaced as leader by a man named Johanan who, in fear of Nebuchadnezzar, asked Jeremiah to seek God regarding the course of action they should take. After ten days God spoke to Jeremiah telling him that the people should not fear, that He would protect them as long as they didn't go to Egypt. If they did, they would be killed by Nebuchadnezzar's army (Jeremiah 42:7-16). Unfortunately, the people rejected God's word and:

> Johanan the son of Kareah and all the captains of the forces took all the remnant of Judah who had returned to dwell in the land of Judah, from all nations where they had been driven-- men, women, children, **the king's daughters**, and every person whom Nebuzaradan the captain of the guard had left with Gedaliah the son of Ahikam, the son of Shaphan, and **Jeremiah the prophet and Baruch the son of Neriah**. So they went to the land of Egypt, for they did not obey the voice of the Lord. And they went as far as Tahpanhes.
> Jeremiah 43:5-7 Emphasis added.

Some say that Jeremiah died in Egypt and others say that he went to Babylon with Nebuchadnezzar's army:

> We have no authentic record of his death. He may have died at Tahpanhes, or, according to a tradition, may have gone to Babylon with the army of Nebuchadnezzar; but of this there is nothing certain.
> — Easton's Illustrated Bible Dictionary

Personally, I believe he went to Babylon before moving on to other locations. One reason I believe he went to Babylon is that Daniel had a copy of Jeremiah's book. See Daniel 9:1-2 where Daniel was reading the books he had and understood Jeremiah's prophecy (Jeremiah 25:11-12;29:10) regarding the seventy years of captivity, and realizing that the seventy years were just about over, started interceding for the captives. I believe that Jeremiah may have personally delivered his book to Daniel, who was a member of Nebuchadnezzar's team of advisors. In either case, he didn't stay in Egypt because he still needed to finish his commission.

While yet in Egypt, God again spoke to Jeremiah:

> Yet a small number who escape the sword shall return from the land of Egypt to the land of Judah; and all the remnant of Judah, who have gone to the land of Egypt to dwell there, shall know whose words will stand, Mine or theirs.
> Jeremiah 44:28

A remnant of those who had gone to Egypt were again to escape and return to the land of Judah.

Baruch was Jeremiah's constant companion and secretary. Please note God's promise of protection to him:

> "Thus says the Lord, the God of Israel, to you, O Baruch: 'You said, "Woe is me now! For the Lord has added grief to my sorrow. I fainted in my sighing, and I find no rest."' Thus you shall say to him, 'Thus says the Lord: "Behold, what I have built I will break down, and what I have planted I will pluck up, that is, this whole land. And do you seek great things for yourself? Do not seek them; for behold, I will bring adversity on all flesh," says the Lord. "But I will give your life to you as a prize in all places, wherever you go."'"
> Jeremiah 45:2-5

Baruch's life as well as Jeremiah's was under divine protection. Jeremiah, Baruch, and the royal seed for replanting and rebuilding David's throne, who were all under God's protection, were to escape, and return to Judah. Then Jeremiah and his group were to travel to a new country which they didn't know.

> **And the remnant who have escaped of the *House of Judah* shall again take root downward, and bear fruit upward.** For out of Jerusalem shall go a remnant, And those who escape from Mount Zion. The zeal of the Lord of hosts will do this.
> Isaiah 37:31-32

Approximately 60 years before Jeremiah's time, Isaiah says the remnant that escapes from Jerusalem will "take root downward," or be replanted, and "bear fruit upward," or be built! The remnant that escaped were Jeremiah and his small band, including Baruch and **Zedekiah's daughters**. But where can we find someone from the tribe of Judah that can rule over at least a portion of Israel to fulfill the promise to David, and to complete the final part of Jeremiah's divine commission?

Chapter 8
The Scarlet Thread and the Breach

To find a member of the tribe of Judah that can carry on the line of David, we need to look at another of those stories in the book of Genesis which we often pass over as "interesting" but of no importance except allegorically. Genesis chapter thirty eight records the birth of Judah's twin sons which he had through his daughter-in-law Tamar.

> Now it came to pass, at the time for giving birth, that behold, twins were in her womb. And so it was, when she was giving birth, that the one put out his hand; and the midwife took a scarlet thread and bound it on his hand, saying, "This one came out first." Then it happened, as he drew back his hand, that his brother came out unexpectedly; and she said, "How did you break through? This breach be upon you!" Therefore his name was called Perez. Afterward his brother came out who had the scarlet thread on his hand. And his name was called Zerah.
> Genesis 38:27-30

Apparently the midwife knew there were twins even before they were born, so she tied a scarlet thread around the hand of the child that put his hand out first so she could tell which would be the firstborn who would be "royal seed" for through him the sceptre promise was to be fulfilled. The child that was actually born first was called "Perez" which means "breach." These births are recorded in detail because there was a reversal of the natural order of things. The one that was expected to be born first actually came out second. I believe God has things recorded in the Bible for a purpose. And this story is here to indicate that eventually this "breach" was to be rectified.

Zerah, of the scarlet thread had five sons (I Chronicles 2:6). The question is, did one of Zerah's descendants finally get the throne in a manner that would heal this breach? David, Zedekiah, and Jesus were all from the Perez branch of Judah, none were from Zerah.

Ezekiel was a contemporary of Jeremiah. He was among the people of Jehoiachin's captivity. Chapter 1 verse 2 refers to the fifth year of Jehoiachin's captivity which would have been about halfway through Zedekiah's reign. Ezekiel was a prophet, not to the *House of Judah*, but to the *House of Israel*. Notice Ezekiel's calling and commission.

> Moreover He said to me, "Son of man, eat what you find; eat this scroll, and go, **speak to the** ***House of Israel***."So I opened my mouth, and He caused me to eat that scroll. And He said to me, "Son of man, feed your belly, and fill your stomach with this scroll that I give you." So I ate, and it was in my mouth like honey in sweetness. Then He said to me: "Son of man, **go to the** ***House of Israel*** and speak with My words to them. For you are not sent to a people of unfamiliar speech and of hard language, but to **the** ***House of Israel***, not to many people of unfamiliar speech and of hard language, whose words you cannot understand. Surely, had I sent you to them, they would have listened to you. But the ***House of Israel*** will not listen to you, because they will not listen to Me; for all **the** *House of Israel* are impudent and hard-hearted. Behold, I have made your face strong against their faces, and your forehead strong against their foreheads. Like adamant stone, harder than flint, I have made your forehead; do not be afraid of them, nor be dismayed at their looks, though they are **a rebellious house**."

Ezekiel 3:1-9 Emphasis added.

Ezekiel's not called primarily to the *House of Judah*, but to the *House of Israel* who God said was "a rebellious house."

Ezekiel records two words that can help us find the answer to where Israel went, and where Jeremiah could plant the royal seed to carry on the dynasty of David. The first part of Ezekiel's 21st chapter is addressed to Jerusalem and the king there who would have been Zedekiah at the time.

> And thou, profane wicked prince of Israel, whose day is come, when iniquity shall have an end, Thus saith the Lord GOD; Remove the diadem, and take off the crown: this shall not be the same: exalt him that is low, and abase him that is high. I will overturn, overturn, overturn, it: and it shall be no more, until he come whose right it is; and I will give it him.
> Ezekiel 21:25-27 (KJV)

Ezekiel is speaking of the diadem and of the crown. These are symbols of the kingly authority, and of the kingly lineage. Ezekiel says there is to be a change, "this shall not be the same." A transformation is to take place. The Zerah line of Judah has been low, while the Perez line has been elevated, and ruling. Now there is to be a change. Exalt him that is low, and abase or humble him that is high. Also, the crown has been in the *House of Judah* and it is to be transferred to the *House of Israel*.

Then Ezekiel mentions three "overturns." Many recent translations, including the New King James don't use this word. Some say "ruin," while others say "overthrown," etc. Some say this is a "Hebrew figure of speech" for emphasis, but that doesn't have to be the case as we shall see. God is going to remove the crown from the exalted line, Perez, and give it to the low, humbled line of Zerah. This is the first overturn from Jerusalem to an undisclosed location. Then will come two more changes of location before it comes to rest, not to be moved again until He comes whose right it is, Jesus the Messiah at his second coming to rule the nations, and God will give it to Him. "The sceptre shall not depart from Judah, nor a lawgiver from between his feet, until Shiloh comes." Now, where will the crown be transferred, and to whom?

Ezekiel's Riddle and Parable

> And the word of the Lord came to me, saying, "Son of man, pose a riddle, and speak a parable to the *House of Israel*,"
> Ezekiel 17:1-2 Emphasis added.

The seventeenth chapter of Ezekiel contains a riddle and a parable that reveal where this diadem/crown is to be taken. The whole chapter is an interesting study and should be read in its entirety, but there are a few important verses. First, the prophecy is not addressed to the *House of Judah*, but it is to give understanding to the lost ten tribes, to the *House of Israel*. The riddle is found in verses 3 to 10. Then beginning in verse 11 we read God's explanation of its meaning.

> Moreover the word of the Lord came to me, saying, "Say now to the rebellious house: 'Do you not know what these things mean?' Tell them, 'Indeed the king of Babylon went to Jerusalem and took its king and princes, and led them with him to Babylon.'"
> Ezekiel 17:11-12

God instructs Ezekiel to talk to "the rebellious house" which is one of the ways God describes the *House of Israel* in his commission given above in Ezekiel 3:1-9. The riddle tells of an eagle coming to Lebanon and taking the highest branch of the cedar, which refers to Nebuchadnezzar who came to Jerusalem to take Jehoiachin, the king of Judah and his children captive to Babylon.

> And he took one of the royal family and made a covenant with him, putting him under oath. He also took away the mighty of the land, that the kingdom might be in subjection, not exalting itself, but keeping his covenant, that it might continue.
> Ezekiel 17:13-14 (NASB)

Nebuchadnezzar took one of the royal family, Jehoiachin's uncle Zedekiah, to be king, making a covenant with him to remain in subjection.

> But he rebelled against him by sending his ambassadors to Egypt, that they might give him horses and many people. Will he prosper? Will he who does such things escape? Can he break a covenant and still be delivered?
> Ezekiel 17:15

Zedekiah rebelled and broke the covenant. The second eagle represents the king of Egypt to whom Zedekiah appealed for help against the Babylonians. God wasn't pleased with this because it showed that Zedekiah despised God's covenant so the kingdom in Judah came to an end (Ezekiel 17:16-21). This is the completion of the first part of Jeremiah's commission to "root out and to pull down" and "to destroy and to throw down." The second part of Jeremiah's commission to "build and to plant" is described in the rest of the chapter containing the parable.

> Thus says the Lord God: "I will take also one of the highest branches of the high cedar and set it out. I will crop off from the topmost of its young twigs a tender one, and will plant it on a high and

prominent mountain. On the mountain height of Israel I will plant it; and it will bring forth boughs, and bear fruit, and be a majestic cedar. Under it will dwell birds of every sort; in the shadow of its branches they will dwell. And all the trees of the field shall know that I, the Lord, have brought down the high tree and exalted the low tree, dried up the green tree and made the dry tree flourish; I, the Lord, have spoken and have done it."
Ezekiel 17:22-24

God says He will remove from the topmost of the branches of the cedar (Zedekiah) "of its young twigs a tender one" (one of Zedekiah's daughters) and He will plant it on a high mountain in Israel where it will bring forth fruit. All the trees, nations, will see it and know what God has done. He has "brought down the high tree and exalted the low tree, dried up the green tree and made the dry tree flourish," that is, brought the Perez line down and exalted the Zerah line. Perez and Judah had been the green tree, but it is now to be dried up; Zerah and Israel are represented by the dry tree which is now to be made to flourish. Jeremiah's commission to build and to plant will be accomplished "on the mountain height of Israel" in the *House of Israel*. Notice again Isaiah 37:31-32 and Ezekiel 21:26 which were quoted earlier:

And the remnant who have escaped of the *House of Judah* shall again take root downward, and bear fruit upward. For out of Jerusalem shall go a remnant, and those who escape from Mount Zion. The zeal of the Lord of hosts will do this.
Isaiah 37:31-32

Thus saith the Lord GOD; Remove the diadem, and take off the crown: this shall not be the same: exalt him that is low, and abase him that is high.
Ezekiel 21:26 (KJV)

Once the princess is taken from the *House of Judah* to the *House of Israel*, she will take root and bear fruit. That is, she will bear offspring who will carry on the lineage of David. The *House of Israel* is now exalted and all the nations will take note of what God has done.

Chapter 9
Where Did the *House of Israel* Go?

There is much evidence showing where the *House of Israel* went after being carried captive by Assyria in 721 B.C., however, there is not space enough to give it all here. The first place to look for information on this subject is, of course, the Bible where we find a number of clues.

The *House of Israel* is called in scripture by several different names in addition to the *House of Israel*. Among them are Ephraim as being the chief tribe of the northern ten tribes, House of Jacob (Jacob said, "Let my name be named on them" meaning Ephraim and Manasseh), Samaria the capital city of the northern tribes, Joseph as being the father of the chief tribes of the ten, etc.

The prophet Amos wrote to the *House of Israel* during the 13th of the 19 kings of the *House of Israel* (Amos 1:1) before the carrying away into captivity. Amos prophesies:

> Behold, the eyes of the Lord God are upon the sinful kingdom [of Israel's ten tribes] and I will destroy it from the surface of the ground, except that I will not utterly destroy the house of Jacob, says the Lord. For behold, I will command, and I will sift the *House of Israel* among all nations and cause it to move to and fro as grain is sifted in a sieve, yet shall not the least kernel fall upon the earth and be lost [from My sight].
> Amos 9:8-9 (AMP)

What is to be destroyed here is the kingdom or government of the ten tribes because of the sins caused by that government, it is not the people that are to be destroyed. The people are to be sifted through the nations, yet God will protect them so that not a kernel will be lost in their travels through the nations. God knows who they are and where they are going. This prophecy is usually applied to the scattered condition of the Jews, but the prophecy itself shows it does not include the Jews of the *House of Judah*, but refers exclusively to the *House of Israel*.

When David wanted to build a house, the temple in Jerusalem, God made the promises referred to earlier that he should have an everlasting dynasty ruling over at least some of the children of Israel. This is recorded in II Samuel 7 and I Chronicles 17. Included in both of these passages is the following statement:

> Moreover I will appoint a place for My people Israel, and will plant them, that they may dwell in a place of their own and move no more.
> I Chronicles 17:9

God says He will plant His people Israel (Jeremiah was commissioned to plant the throne among them). Because of the context, it is evident that He is not referring to Palestine as the whole twelve tribes of the *House of Israel*, and the *House of Judah* were already dwelling there and would later be removed. It has to refer to another land where the scattered *House of Israel* would gather after that scattering and sifting. Then they were to "move no more" once they reached this place of their own.

> Ephraim feeds on the wind, And pursues the east wind.
> Hosea 12:1

An east wind travels west. If Ephraim pursues the east wind, then we would find them west of Jerusalem.

> Also I will set his hand over the sea, And his right hand over the rivers.
> Psalm 89:25

Psalm 89 is one of the places where it is recorded that God promised David a perpetual dynasty. Verse 25 prophesies rulership over the sea, the hand representing authority.

> Then the Lord said to me, "Backsliding Israel has shown herself more righteous than treacherous Judah. Go and proclaim these words toward the north, and say: 'Return, backsliding Israel,' says the Lord; 'I will not cause My anger to fall on you. For I am merciful,' says the Lord; 'I will not remain angry forever.'"
> Jeremiah 3:11-12

Israel had lived north of Jerusalem before being carried into captivity, but at the time of Jeremiah, some 140 years later, he is told to say to them "Go and proclaim these words toward the north." Israel had been carried captive and God said you could find them in the north. They had long ago migrated with the Assyrians, north (and west) of Assyria's original location.

> Listen, O isles, unto me; and hearken, ye people, from far. . . Thou art my servant, O Israel, in whom I will be glorified.
> Isaiah 49:1, 3 (KJV)

> Behold, these shall come from far: and, lo, these from the north and from the west; and these from the land of Sinim.
> Isaiah 49:12 (KJV)

Isaiah is prophesying of a time when the *House of Israel* will return to the land originally given to Abraham. God told him to speak to a people who dwell in the isles, (some translations say coastlands, or islands). In Hebrew there is no compound word for northwest as we have in English, so the prophet says these people will come from the north and from the west, indicating the

northwest direction from Jerusalem. If you take a map and draw
a line directly northwest of Jerusalem you will come to what is
called on modern maps, "the British Isles" which is today called
The United Kingdom, meaning Ireland, Scotland, and England.
The only people living in isles in the sea and directly northwest
of Jerusalem is the people of the British Isles. Jeremiah confirms
that Israel was dwelling in the isles during his ministry.

> I am a Father to Israel, and Ephraim is My
> firstborn. "Hear the word of the Lord, O nations,
> And declare it in the isles afar off, and say,'He
> who scattered Israel will gather him, And keep
> him as a shepherd does his flock.'"
> Jeremiah 31:9b-10

Jeremiah was told to tell Israel and Ephraim in the isles afar
off that He would gather Israel and protect him like a shepherd.
If you read the entire 31st chapter of Jeremiah it is easy to see who
the people are who are being addressed. In verse 5 Samaria is
mentioned, verse 6 speaks of the mountains of Ephraim, verse 7
refers to "the remnant of Israel," and verse 8 says they will come
from the north country and from the ends of the earth.

That the descendants of Joseph should be a people who spread
out from their homeland is evident from the prophecy of dying
Israel when he prophesied over each of his twelve sons in Genesis
chapter 49:

> Joseph is a fruitful bough, a fruitful bough by a
> well; his branches run over the wall.
> Genesis 49:22

This can have various meanings, but when taken nationally
according to the birthright promise it is obvious that Joseph,
meaning Ephraim and Manasseh, will be expansive and "his
branches," or children, will "run over the wall," or expand beyond
their borders. One of, if not the most colonizing people in the

history of the world has been the British people, Ephraim, who are headquartered in the British Isles.

> When the Most High divided their inheritance to the nations, when He separated the sons of Adam, He set the boundaries of the peoples according to the number of the children of Israel.
> Deuteronomy 32:8

This scripture tells us that when God set the boundaries for all the nations, He first looked at the number He had planned for the sons of Israel, and made room for them before dividing the rest of the earth. It also tells us that God expected there to be more Israelites than would be able to fit into the area called the "Promised Land," considering that the sons of Joseph, Ephraim and Manasseh, were prophesied to expand over their borders like a fruitful vine.

Chapter 10
A Summary

So far we have studied Abraham, Isaac, and Jacob the patriarchs of scripture, the progenitors of the nations of Israel, the *House of Israel* to the north, and the *House of Judah* to the south. We followed the split between the birthright promises and the sceptre promises into these two houses. In Genesis chapter 48 we saw the birthright pass to Joseph when Israel adopted Joseph's two Egyptian born sons, Ephraim and Manasseh, and in chapter 49 we saw the sceptre promise given to Judah.

We also learned of the unusual circumstances surrounding the birth of Judah's twin sons Perez and Zerah. The line of David came from Perez while the son of the scarlet thread, Zerah, was left out, a "breach" having been created.

We saw the throne of a united Israel given to David, then we learned about God's unconditional promise to David that he would always have a descendant sitting on a throne, ruling over at least a portion of Israel

Then the *House of Israel* was invaded by the Assyrians starting in 734 B.C. then conquered and taken captive beginning in 721 to 718 B.C. They were carried north by the Assyrians to be lost from the view of everyone but God who would sift them among the nations, and those to whom He would reveal them. The *House of Judah* was invaded and taken captive by Nebuchadnezzar king of Babylon beginning around 604 B.C. during the ministry of Jeremiah. Jerusalem finally fell to the Babylonians in 585 B.C.

In Jeremiah's commission God said He was going to accomplish several things, including "to root out and to pull down, to destroy and to throw down" the kingdom or government of Judah and then to take part of the "royal seed" from the Perez line of Judah in the form of "the king's daughters" from the *House of Judah* to the *House of Israel* where he would meet up with a member of the Zerah line of Judah **so the unconditional**

promise God had made to David of a perpetual dynasty would be kept.

We have located the *House of Israel* in the isles due northwest of Jerusalem. We see this from multiple sources, including Isaiah, Amos, Hosea, and significantly Jeremiah who would have to take these princesses to repair the breach between Perez and Zerah, the illegitimate sons of Judah.

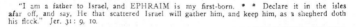

"I am a father to Israel, and EPHRAIM is my first-born. * * Declare it in the isles afar off, and say, He that scattered Israel will gather him, and keep him, as a shepherd doth his flock." Jer. 31: 9, 10.

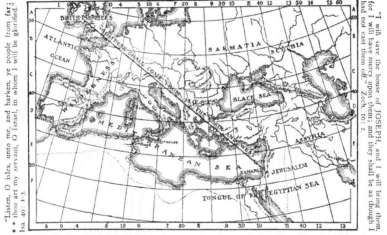

"Behold these (Israel in the isles) shall come from far, and lo, these from the north and from the west. The children which thou shalt have, *after thou hast lost the other*, shall say again in thine ears, The place is too strait (cramped) for me, give a place to me that I may dwell. Isa. 49: 12, 20.
EPHRAIM—ISRAEL IN THE ISLES.

Chapter 11
Corroborating Evidence

In any court of law evidence is presented to show the main argument and to support the conclusion and then additional, or corroborating evidence is presented which supports the original conclusion. We are now ready to review such corroborating evidence. There are many such pieces of evidence presented in detail in different works on the subject, but only some of them can be presented here.

Hebrew Names of Britain
The Hebrew word for "covenant" as listed in Strong's dictionary is: "berit"

> Hebrew Strong's Number: 1285 ב·ר,תי
> Transliteration: berît
> from <H1262> (barah) (in the sense of cutting [like <H1254> (bara')]); a compact (because made by passing between pieces of flesh) :- confederacy, [con-]feder[-ate], covenant, league.
> — Strong's Talking Greek & Hebrew Dictionary

Other Hebrew dictionaries spell it as *beriyt* or *beriyth*. After Gideon died, Israel followed the pagan god Baal. In Judges 8:33 and 9:4 the word "covenant" is used as a proper name connected with "Baal." This is transliterated by several translations as "Baalberith" or as "Baal-Berith." The Message Bible translates it as "Baal-of-the-Covenant."

> So it was, as soon as Gideon was dead, that the children of Israel again played the harlot with the Baals, and made Baal-Berith their god.
> Judges 8:33

The Hebrew word for "man" is *iysh*, or *ish* (See #376 in Strong's Hebrew dictionary). In English, the suffix "-ish" means "*of or belonging to* (a person or nation)." In ancient Hebrew there are never any vowels given when writing. Later Hebrew has "vowel pointers," but the vowels are not written. Thus, leaving out the "e" from *berith*, but retaining the "I" to retain the "y" sound in its anglicized form we have the anglicized Hebrew word for covenant, "*brith* or *brit*." It was a proclivity of Ephraimites to never pronounce their "h's" (see Judges 12:5-6) as is also the case in parts of modern Britain, so the anglicized form of the Hebrew word for covenant would be pronounced *brit*. The word for "covenant man" or "covenant people" in Hebrew would be simply, "Brit-ish." Can it be a coincidence that the true covenant people, holders of the birthright passed from Abraham to Isaac, then to Jacob and finally to Ephraim and Manasseh, sons of Jacob's favorite son Joseph, are called the "British" and that they live in the "British Isles"?

God told Abraham, "in Isaac shall thy seed be called" (Genesis 21:12. Romans 9:7, Hebrews 11:18). The Hebrew word for "called" is #7121 in Strong's Hebrew Dictionary and means to name something. It can also mean "calling to a specific task." So God is telling Abraham that his seed or the recipients of the birthright promise would be named or called in Isaac. In Amos 7:16, the *House of Israel* is called "the House of Isaac." (See Amos 7:10) They were the descendants of Isaac and are therefore Isaac's sons. If you drop the "I" from Isaac, as it is not used when spelling in Hebrew, you have the modern name "Saac's Sons", or as it is spelled today, "Saxons."

Signposts and Waymarks

God intended for the *House of Israel* to be found and not to remain lost forever. If this is true, then we should find indicators along the way showing where these people migrated after they were taken into captivity. Through the prophet Jeremiah God told Ephraim (See Jeremiah 31:20):

> Set up signposts, make landmarks; set your heart
> toward the highway, the way in which you went.
> Turn back, O virgin of Israel, turn back to these
> your cities.
> Jeremiah 31:21

The tribe of Dan was a part of the *House of Israel.* There are some interesting things to note about this tribe, starting with Israel's deathbed prophecy regarding Dan.

> Dan shall be a serpent by the way, A viper by the
> path,
> Genesis 49:17

Some suggest that another way to translate this is "Dan shall be a serpent's trail," but I can find no translation where it is so translated. Adam Clark's commentary on this verse says, "The word חרא orach, which we translate path, signifies the track or rut made in the ground by the wheel of a cart, wagon, etc." suggesting that a path, a rut or track is being created on the way and we find Dan there, so I am comfortable with Dan being a Serpent's trail. Let's see how this works out. Significantly, the tribe of Dan had the proclivity of naming places after Dan their tribal father. For example:

> And the border of the children of Dan went
> beyond these, because the children of Dan went
> up to fight against Leshem and took it; and they
> struck it with the edge of the sword, took
> possession of it, and dwelt in it. They called
> Leshem, Dan, after the name of Dan their father.
> Joshua 19:47

> And six hundred men of the family of the Danites
> went from there, from Zorah and Eshtaol, armed
> with weapons of war. Then they went up and

encamped in Kirjath Jearim in Judah. (Therefore they call that place Mahaneh Dan to this day. There it is, west of Kirjath Jearim.)
Judges 18:11-12

And they called the name of the city Dan, after the name of Dan their father, who was born to Israel. However, the name of the city formerly was Laish.
Judges 18:29

First they took a city called Leshem and renamed it Dan. Later they called a place Mahaneh Dan, literally camp of Dan (margin). Later the six hundred men took Laish and renamed the city Dan in Judges 18:29. This became the northernmost part of the land of Israel. We read of the land extending from Dan to Beer-sheeba, from the north to the south. So the Danites left a trail or set up waymarks or signposts for us to trace them today. Don't forget that in Hebrew only the consonants were written, so Dan would be represented by the letters DN. When transliterated into another language, we might find "Dan," or "Den," or "Din," or "Don," or "Dun" and it comes from the same Hebrew name.

From Judges 5:17 we discover that at least part the tribe of Dan was a seafaring tribe (see Adam Clark's and the Jamieson-Fausset- Brown commentaries). Before the Assyrian invasion the tribe of Dan occupied two separate districts in the Holy Land, one group living on the seacoast and were principally seamen, while the other group lived more inland. When Assyria captured Israel, the seafaring Danites escaped in their ships, traveling west and north along the shores of the Mediterranean sea where they left their trail of "Den," "Don," and "Dun."

Irish annals and history tell of a people coming in ships to settle Ireland called the "Tuatha de Dannans," which being translated means, "Tribe of Dan" or "People of Dan." Sometimes the name appears as "Tuatha De" meaning "people of God." This group is sometimes associated with a female deity named "Danu." Normally, we should have a problem with this, but remember that the *House of Israel* was driven from their land because of idolatry which started during the days of the Judges or before and which intensified following the split between the *House of Israel* and the kingdom of Rehoboam, Solomon's son. When Jeroboam became king of the *House of Israel* he became fearful of losing his power instead of having faith in God's plain promise so he set up idols for the people in two cities, Bethel and Dan (I Kings 12:25). The tribe of Dan was one of the first on record to set up idol worship in the Promised Land.

In Ireland the "Tribe of Dan" left their "waymarks" such as "*Dans*-Laugh, *Don*-Sower, *Dun*-dalk, *Dun*-drum, *Don*-egal City, *Dun*-glow, *Din*-gle, *Dun*smore (which means "more Dans"). Incidentally, the name Dunn in Irish means the same as Dan in Hebrew, "judge."

The northern colony of Dan was taken captive to Assyria and from there, with the rest of the ten tribes, traveled from Assyria by land. After leaving Assyrian captivity, they lived just west of the Black Sea where we find the rivers *Dni*eper, *Dni*ster, and the *Don*.

In either ancient or later geography, we find these waymarks; *Dan*-au, the *Dan*-inn, the *Dun*-raven, the *Dan*-ube river the *Dan*-aster, the *Dan*-dari, the *Dan*-ez, the *Don*, the *Dan*, and the U-*Don*, the Eri-*don*, even to the *Danes* dwelling in the country of Denmark, which means "Dan's mark." Upon arriving in the British Isles, the tribe of Dan set up additional "waymark" names such as *Dun*-dee, *Dun*-raven, etc. In Scotland the "Dans," "Dons," and "Duns" are as common as they are in Ireland. In addition, consider the Scan-*din*-avian countries: Denmark; Finland; Iceland; Norway; Sweden. While it is beyond the scope of this book, evidence exists showing the modern identities of each of the "Lost Tribes of Israel" including those dwelling in the Scandinavian countries. (See Appendix C)

Dan truly left their "serpent's trail" by setting up waymarks that lead directly from the Middle East to the British Isles.

Ireland's Ancient Records

Ireland has a long history recorded in ancient annals, legends, and histories. With Bible history and prophecy as a guide, it is possible to leave out what is obviously legend and myth from the true history of Ireland. We have already seen the story of the "Tuatha de Dannan" when discussing the waymarks left by the Tribe of Dan. This group arrived in ships as a strong colony long prior to 700 B.C. They drove out other tribes and settled there. It has been said that later, during the time of David, a group from the line of Zerah arrived in Ireland from the Near East.

In 569 B.C. (the time of Jeremiah transplanting), an elderly patriarch came to Ireland who one author connects with a man named "Iarbanel (or Larbanel) the Prophet" who was Jeremiah "son of God," "Iar" being a shortened form of the name Jeremiah, "ban or ben" being Hebrew for son, and "El" being one of the Hebrew names of God. He is referred to as a "saint," and as a "prophet." He brought with him the princess daughter of an eastern king and a companion named "Simon Brach," with various spellings in different histories as Breck, Berach, Berech, or Brach. The princess had a Hebrew name Tephi, her full name being Tea-Tephi. Some confuse this Tea-Tephi, one of Zedekiah's daughters, with an earlier Tea, who lived during the time of David.

Some references I have checked state that the party included the son of the king of Ireland who had been in Jerusalem during the siege where he met Tea-Tephi. They were married shortly after 585 B.C. when Jerusalem fell. Some also tell of their young son of about 12 years who accompanied them to Ireland. Some of these references state that Jeremiah brought some other items, including the harp, and a stone called "lia-fail" or "stone of destiny." This stone deserves its own section as it is a fascinating artifact.

The Stone of Destiny - Lia-Fail

Lia-Fail or The Stone of Destiny

I know of no people, other than the British, Scottish, and Irish people who possess a stone that has such a rich history. From 1296 until 1996 there was a stone in the bottom of the coronation chair in Westminster Abby. In 1996 it was returned to the city of Scone, Scotland where it resides in Edinburgh Castle. The history of this stone goes all the way back to ancient Ireland. It is called by several names, including the Stone of Destiny, the Stone of Scone, and "lia-fail." Coincidentally, Hebrew reads from right to left, and English reads from left to right. When you read this name in either direction, it is still "lia-fail."

For centuries kings and queens of Ireland, Scotland and England were inaugurated or crowned on or near this stone. There is also an interesting stone mentioned in the pages of the Bible.

> Moreover, brethren, I do not want you to be unaware that all our fathers were under the cloud, all passed through the sea, all were baptized into Moses in the cloud and in the sea, all ate the same spiritual food, and all drank the same spiritual

drink. For they drank of that spiritual Rock that
followed them, and that Rock was Christ.
1 Corinthians 10:1-4

Several things are mentioned in this scripture. First, the cloud,
second the baptism in the sea, then the manna, which Jesus said
represented Him, and finally the rock that they drank from which
Paul says was Christ. I always thought from sermons I heard that
Paul was speaking of a figurative rock, but since the other items
mentioned were real occurrences or objects further study shows
that there was very likely a physical rock that went with the
Children of Israel during their journeys which represented Christ.
Almost everything in the Old Testament represented spiritual
truth which is revealed in the New Testament.

The story of this rock begins with Jacob before his name was
changed to Israel. Jacob obtained the blessing from his father
Isaac and then he left his home in fear of his brother Esau.
Genesis chapter 28 tells the story. As Jacob traveled from
Beersheeba to Haran, he stopped for the night in "a certain place"
to sleep. He took a stone and used it as a pillow. During the night
he had a dream of angels ascending and descending on a "ladder"
or a staircase. In this dream Jacob was given the promises referred
to already in which God promised him the blessings of Abraham
and Isaac. He also received promises of protection on his journey
to and from Haran.

Then Jacob awoke from his sleep and said,
"Surely the Lord is in this place, and I did not
know it" And he was afraid and said, "How
awesome is this place! **This is none other than
the house of God**, and this is the gate of heaven!"

Then Jacob rose early in the morning, and took
the stone that he had put at his head, set it up as a
pillar, and poured oil on top of it. **And he called
the name of that place Bethel**; but the name of

that city had been Luz previously. Then Jacob
made a vow, saying, "If God will be with me, and
keep me in this way that I am going, and give me
bread to eat and clothing to put on, so that I come
back to my father's house in peace, then the Lord
shall be my God. **And this stone which I have
set as a pillar shall be God's house**, and of all
that You give me I will surely give a tenth to
You."
Genesis 28:16-22 Emphasis added.

Sometimes you hear that Jacob was bargaining with God by
promising to pay a tithe to get Him to keep His promises, but
more likely, Jacob was saying, "If you are going to do all this for
me, the least I can do is give you a tenth of everything."

Regardless of that, notice that Jacob called both the place he
stopped and the stone he used as a pillow and set up as a pillar,
"the house of God," which in Hebrew is Bethel. Both the place
and the stone are called Bethel in that sense. During the Exodus
there are two instances where the people drank from a rock as was
mentioned by Paul in I Corinthians 10.

And the Lord said to Moses, "Go on before the
people, and take with you some of the elders of
Israel. Also take in your hand your rod with which
you struck the river, and go. Behold, I will stand
before you there on the rock in Horeb; and you
shall strike **the** rock, and water will come out of it,
that the people may drink." And Moses did so in
the sight of the elders of Israel.
Exodus 17:5-6 Emphasis added.

God did not say that Moses was to find a rock, nor did God tell
him to strike "that" rock, but He told him to strike "the" rock, a
particular rock that Moses and the Israelites already knew about.
This is also true in the second instance:

Then the Lord spoke to Moses, saying, "Take the rod; you and your brother Aaron gather the congregation together. Speak to **the** rock before their eyes, and it will yield its water; thus you shall bring water for them out of **the** rock, and give drink to the congregation and their animals." Numbers 20:7-8 Emphasis added.

God told Moses to take "the" rod. He didn't have to explain which rod He meant. There was only one rod Moses used. In the same way, God said to speak to "the" rock and it would produce its water for the people to drink. Unfortunately for Moses, he let his anger get the best of him and he "lifted his hand and struck the rock twice with his rod" (verse 11), for which Moses was not allowed to go into the Promised Land because the Rock, who was Christ, was to be struck only once for the salvation of mankind and that had symbolically already been done.

Later you read about a *pilla*r in the book of II Kings. Remember, Jacob used this rock as a pillow, and then set it up for a *pillar* and anointed it with oil before God. In the eleventh chapter of II Kings is the story of Athaliah who, upon the death of her son Ahaziah wanted to sit on the throne of David, and had all the "royal seed" killed and she took the throne. However, Jehosheba took Ahaziah's young son Joash and hid him in the temple for six years. When Joash was eight years old Jehoida gathered together the rulers and captains to a coronation ceremony. When Athaliah heard the noise, she went to the temple to find out what was going on.

When Athaliah heard the noise made by the guards and the people, she went to the people at the temple of the LORD. She looked and there was the king, standing by **the** pillar, **as the custom was**. The officers and the trumpeters were beside the king, and all the people of the land were rejoicing and blowing trumpets. Then

> Athaliah tore her robes and called out, "Treason!
> Treason!"
> 2 Kings 11:13-14 (NIV) Emphasis added.

The King James and New King James versions of the Bible read that the king was standing by "a" pillar, but most other translations I checked say "the" pillar, meaning a specific pillar that was used in coronation ceremonies "as the custom was."

In the twenty second chapter of II Kings is recorded the story of the book of the Law being found in the cleansing of the temple during the days of king Josiah. Then in the twenty third chapter, this same pillar is mentioned again when Josiah renewed the covenant the *House of Judah* had forsaken for many years.

> The king stood by **the** pillar and renewed the covenant in the presence of the LORD--to follow the LORD and keep his commands, regulations and decrees with all his heart and all his soul, thus confirming the words of the covenant written in this book. Then all the people pledged themselves to the covenant.
> 2 Kings 23:3 (NIV) Emphasis added.

Again, the King James and New King James translations say "a" pillar, but the NIV and most other translations state that the king stood by "the" pillar.

Now, back to England. The coronation stone mentioned at the beginning of this section has had a long history. For many years, it sat under the coronation chair in Westminster Abby, where a plaque hung next to it proclaiming it to be "Jacob's Pillow Stone." Irish history indicates that Jeremiah brought this stone to Ireland with him when he brought the royal seed. For many years the Stone of Destiny remained in Ireland's palace of Taragh, upon which kings and queens of Ireland were crowned. The stone was taken to Scotland by King Fergus Mor Mac Earca who, upon that stone, became King of Scotland around the year 498 A.D. The stone and the throne were moved, overturned, from Ireland to Scotland.

In 1296 A. D. the English king Edward I captured the stone and the kingdom was once again overturned, this time from Scotland to England. Due to marriages between the families of the kings of Ireland, Scotland, and England over the centuries, the dynasty of kings continued unbroken from the time of the arrival of Jeremiah and his band shortly after 585 B.C. until now. The last monarch to be crowned upon the Stone of Destiny was Queen Elizabeth II who is the current Queen of England. These kings and queens all come from the marriage between members of the Perez and Zerah lines of Israel's son Judah, thus David still has a descendant sitting on the throne ruling over at least a portion of the *House of Israel*.

We can see Ezekiel's three overturns of the throne of David from the *House of Judah* to the *House of Israel* being first from Jerusalem to Ireland, then from Ireland to Scotland, and finally from Scotland to England. The Stone of Destiny was returned in 1996 to Scotland's Edinburgh Castle, perhaps for safe keeping, but the throne of David remains in England. If we ever see the British throne moved from England back to Jerusalem, we can be sure that Shiloh is about to come, whose right it is. Everyone who knows anything about Christmas has heard these words:

> Then the angel said to her, "Do not be afraid, Mary, for you have found favor with God. And behold, you will conceive in your womb and bring forth a Son, and shall call His name Jesus. He will be great, and will be called the Son of the Highest; and the Lord God will give Him the throne of His father David. And He will reign over the house of Jacob forever, and of His kingdom there will be no end."
> Luke 1:30-33

This overturn of the throne of David back to Jerusalem has to happen at or shortly after the *House of Israel* and the *House of Judah* are once again a single kingdom. This will take place in connection with the return of Christ to establish his government on the earth. (Ezekiel 37:15-28)

Anyone who knows the history of the British people surely understands by now that the promises made to Joseph's son Ephraim that he should be "a company of nations" has been fulfilled in that people. What was once the British Empire, upon which the sun never set, has become the British Commonwealth of Nations, the only such "company of nations" in the history of the earth. But the first colony the British Empire created was called "New England" in the "new world." Within about one hundred and fifty years New England had a dispute with the king of England and through its Revolutionary War separated into a new nation called The United States of America. Significantly, the dispute which resulted in the American Revolutionary War was, to a great extent, brought on because of the way the British crown treated the colonies, and taxation. These are the very same issues which caused the separation of the *House of Israel* from the *House of Judah* during the days of Solomon's son Rehoboam.

The Founders of the United States, when devising the new government, chose People's Law as practiced by the Anglo-Saxons to be their pattern. Significantly, they noticed the similarities between the government of the Anglo-Saxons and the Ancient people of Israel. Can it be a coincidence that these two people groups had the same basic structure? (See Appendix F for further explanation)

Chapter 12
Where is Manasseh?

In order to understand the connection of The United States of America with the tribe of Manasseh, it is necessary to look at the tribes of Israel in a little more detail.

It is commonly believed that there are 12 tribes in Israel. This is true to a point. In actual fact, there are 13 tribes, although there is only mention of 12 at any one time. One thing God has done more than once is start with twelve, then add one while taking away another to still come back to twelve. A good example is the twelve disciples of our Lord Jesus Christ whom He named apostles. One of these betrayed Him and was disqualified from holding the office and fulfilling the commission. This was Judas who betrayed Jesus. After the resurrection and ascension of Jesus, the apostle Peter called for a casting of lots to fill the empty office.

> And they cast their lots, and the lot fell on
> Matthias. And he was numbered with the eleven
> apostles.
> Acts 1:26

Some say this was unnecessary because the apostle Paul was chosen by God to fulfill that position. However, that cannot be the case because the original twelve were given a different commission than was Paul. (See Appendix E for further detail)

When we are talking about the tribes of Israel, we need to recognize that the same thing happened. Jacob had twelve sons and one daughter. The daughter is not counted because no tribe came from her. When Israel adopted the two sons of Joseph in Genesis chapter 48, there became thirteen tribes. Joseph was counted as one of the twelve tribes, until Ephraim took his place when he received the larger portion of the birthright blessing along with his older brother, Manasseh. This made Manasseh the thirteenth tribe (see Revelation 7:4-8 where the tribe of Manasseh and the tribe of Joseph are mentioned with Joseph standing in for Ephraim). We then come back to twelve in the division of the Promised Land because one tribe is left out. The tribe of Levi was not given an inheritance, a specific plot of land for their dwelling, but were scattered throughout the other tribes in order to minister the ordinances and the law of the Lord to all the tribes. So the number thirteen is strongly associated with Manasseh.

When we look at the United States, we see the number thirteen stamped all over it as well. There were thirteen original colonies which later became the original thirteen states. Just as the British coat of arms (see Appendix D) is directly connected with Ephraim so also, the Great Seal of the United States reflects the Israelite origins of this nation, and specifically points to the tribe of Manasseh. Ephraim became the company of nations while Manasseh became the one single great nation God promised to the children of Joseph.

Some look at the seal of the United States as depicted on the one dollar bill and see a lot of pagan symbolism with Masonic origins. However, there is another reasonable explanation. God inspired the founding fathers in the design of the seal. Before we can go there, we need to answer a few questions.

First of all, if Britain is Ephraim and the United States is Manasseh, why doesn't the world recognize them as Israelites instead of thinking of them as "Gentiles?" For the same reason the sons of Israel didn't recognize Joseph when they met him face to face upon their arrival in Egypt looking for food. Joseph looked Egyptian! He looked like a pagan even though he was a believer in, and the chief instrument of the God of Israel to the world of his day. By the time the sons of Israel arrived, Joseph had lost his youthful look and now dressed like an Egyptian. In addition, there were four different mothers for the twelve sons of Jacob, so they would have different DNA and different family traits. To add to that, the mother of Ephraim and Manasseh was Egyptian. They would look totally different than, say, the sons of Judah, or the sons of Levi.

There is a second reason and that has to do with the sin of the northern ten tribes of the *House of Israel*. Remember that when Jeroboam became king of the northern tribes, he became fearful that if the people went to Jerusalem to worship, they would eventually abandon him and return to the king in Judah. Therefore, he did two things that caused the *House of Israel* to lose the sign which would show that it is a part of Israel when it was taken captive. In fact it was for this very reason that they were taken captive in the first place.

The first thing Jeroboam did was to set up gold calves in the cities of Dan and Bethel for the *House of Israel* to worship. The second thing he did was to change the dates of the annual high holy days so the people would not go to Jerusalem and be tempted to return to the kingdom under David's house. (I Kings 12:25-33). Along with that, the *House of Israel* ceased to observe the Sabbath day as God had ordained. There was a separate covenant that God made with Israel regarding the Sabbath so it would be a sign by which they would retain the knowledge of God as the creator. It also serves to identify the people of God to the world.

> "Speak also to the children of Israel, saying: 'Surely My Sabbaths you shall keep, for it is a sign between Me and you throughout your generations, that you may know that I am the Lord who sanctifies you.
> Exodus 31:13

> "'Therefore the children of Israel shall keep the Sabbath, to observe the Sabbath throughout their generations as a perpetual covenant. It is a sign between Me and the children of Israel forever; for in six days the Lord made the heavens and the earth, and on the seventh day He rested and was refreshed.'"
> Exodus 31:16-17

A separate covenant was made between God and Israel regarding the Sabbath which became a "sign" between God and the people. The *House of Israel* was driven out of the land due to these two things, idolatry and Sabbath breaking. Once the *House of Judah* saw what happened, they became very strict in their Sabbath observance so that Jesus had to tell the people, "The Sabbath was made for man, and not man for the Sabbath." (Mark 2:27) Apart from the fact that some of the Jews returned to Jerusalem, people recognize the Jews as Israel because of their observance of the Sabbaths, the weekly and annual Sabbath days.

So, the world doesn't recognize the United States and Britain as being of Israelite heritage because they don't "look" Israelite because of their physical appearance, and because they don't practice the Jewish religion, factors that should be expected in the "Ten Lost Tribes" of the *House of Israel*.

The Great Seal of The United States

Now, let's look at the seal of the United States as it appears on the back of the one dollar bill. This seal has two sides, the front of which shows an eagle with an olive branch in one talon and arrows in the other. The olive branch is a symbol of the tribe of Joseph, a secondary symbol being arrows. In the seal, the arrows are the symbol of military might. Notice what Jacob/Israel said regarding Joseph:

> "Joseph is a fruitful bough, a fruitful bough by a well; his branches run over the wall. The archers have bitterly grieved him, shot at him and hated him. But his bow remained in strength, and the arms of his hands were made strong by the hands of the Mighty God of Jacob."
> Genesis 49:22-24

First he says Joseph is fruitful and will expand. Then he says he will have enemies who hate him and will take shots at him, but he will have strong weapons because the Mighty God of Jacob would make him strong. This can mean none other than the people of Ephraim and Manasseh, the people of Britain and the United States. It can also be noted that on the Great Seal of the United States, the eagle is facing the olive branch, meaning peace is the aim, but once forced into war, the face of the eagle turns to the arrows, because he isn't afraid to use the power given by God. Regarding "the archers (who) have bitterly grieved him, shot at him and hated him," read the words of Jesus in His answer to the disciples' questions about the time of the end:

> "Then they will deliver you up to tribulation and kill you, **and you will be hated by all nations for My name's sake**."
> Matthew 24:9 Emphasis added.

There are three nations on the earth today that are hated more than any other nation, and it is primarily for "My name's sake," the name of the God of Abraham, Isaac, and Jacob. Those nations are the Jewish nation called Israel in the middle east, Britain, and the United States of America, three brother nations. It is no coincidence that Ephraim and Manasseh are the greatest supporters of the Jewish nation, and are primarily responsible for its existence as a nation. These brother nations have been shot at and grieved by their enemies, but their military has remained strong by the favor of God.

The eagle on this seal is also of special significance. God spoke to the people of Israel likening Himself to an eagle.

> "You have seen what I did to the Egyptians, and how **I bore you on eagles' wings** and brought you to Myself."
> Exodus 19:4 Emphasis added.

> "For the Lord's portion is His people; Jacob is the place of His inheritance. He found him in a desert land and in the wasteland, a howling wilderness;

He encircled him, He instructed him, He kept him as the apple of His eye. **As an eagle stirs up its nest**, hovers over its young, spreading out its wings, taking them up, carrying them on its wings, so the Lord alone led him, and there was no foreign god with him."
Deuteronomy 32:9-12 Emphasis added.

It was God who stirred up the nest of the *House of Israel* and carried them to their new homeland.

The number thirteen figures prominently on the front of the seal as follows:

- 13 stars in the glory cloud above the eagle (formed in the shape of a Star of David)
- 13 stripes in the shield
- 13 olive leaves
- 13 olives
- 13 arrows
- 13 feathers in the arrows
- 13 letters in E Pluribus Unum

Looking at the reverse side of the Great Seal of the United States, we see a pyramid of 13 rows of stones. In place of the capstone, is the eye of the Almighty. In a pyramid, the chief cornerstone is the stone which appears at the top. It is no coincidence that there is no top stone on the Great Pyramid in the land of Egypt and, referring to Christ, three of the four gospel writers quote Jesus speaking of a rejected cornerstone.

> Jesus said to them, "Have you never read in the Scriptures: 'The stone which the builders rejected Has become the chief cornerstone. This was the Lord's doing, And it is marvelous in our eyes'?"
> Matthew 21:42

Have you not even read this Scripture: "The stone which the builders rejected Has become the chief cornerstone."
Mark 12:10

Then He looked at them and said, "What then is this that is written: 'The stone which the builders rejected Has become the chief cornerstone'?"
Luke 20:17

The "all seeing eye" at the top of the Pyramid isn't a pagan symbol at all. We need to recognize that Satan doesn't invent anything, but he copies and counterfeits it in order to make the people of God avoid it. We need to stop allowing ourselves to be intimidated by Satan so we won't recognize what is actually of God just because Satan has twisted it to his own purposes.

So, then the pyramid on the back of the Great Seal ties the tribe of Manasseh back to their origins in Egypt where they had an Egyptian mother and an Israelite father, Joseph, who worshiped and served the God of Abraham, Isaac, and Israel. The number 13 is also present on the back of the seal as follows:

- 13 letters in Annuit Coeptis
- 13 courses of stone in the Pyramid

One other thing appears on the back of the Great Seal of the United States, a banner proclaiming the words, "Novo Ordo Seclorum." There are some who say that this means "New World Order" and refers to a conspiracy beginning in 1776 to create a one world government. The truth is only found by understanding the source of this phrase. I quote from a web site listed in the bibliography:

"Novus Ordo Seclorum" was the motto suggested in 1782 by Charles Thomson, the Founding Father chosen by the Continental Congress to come up with the final design for the Great Seal of the United States.

On June 20, 1782, Congress approved Thomson's design for both sides of the Great Seal whose official description states:

**"On the base of the pyramid the numerical letters
MDCCLXXVI
& underneath the following motto. 'novus ordo seclorum'."**

He put the motto at the bottom of the reverse side where its meaning ties into the imagery above it: the unfinished pyramid with the date MDCCLXXVI (1776).

Thomson did not provide an exact translation of the motto, but he explained its symbolism: Novus Ordo Seclorum signifies **"the beginning of the new American Æra,"** which commences from 1776.

The Great Seal of the United States

Chapter 13
2520 Year Wait for the Birthright

The two mightiest powers in world history showed up suddenly on the scene – one a commonwealth of nations forming the greatest empire of all time; the other, the wealthiest, most powerful nation in history. This end time, sudden growth to world prominence was the fulfillment of Bible prophecy.

In Leviticus chapter 26, the 12 tribe nation of Israel was given the promise that if they followed God's civil statutes, obeyed His commandments and ordinances, they should inherit the great national promises of the birthright. These promises included everything needed to produce wealth and prosperity.

But starting in verse 14 God spoke to them about what would happen if they disobeyed. They would become slaves of other nations and go into national punishment with the birthright being withheld for 2520 years.

> And after all this, if you do not obey Me, then I
> will punish you seven times more for your sins.
> Leviticus 26:18

The expression "seven times" is translated from the Hebrew word *shibah* which has a dual meaning. It can mean "seven times" and also "sevenfold" (see number 7651 in Strong's Hebrew dictionary). The "seven times" indicates duration or continuation of punishment, but the word also implies seven times greater intensity of punishment. It is used this way in Daniel 3:19 where King Nebuchadnezzar commanded that the furnace Daniel's three friends were thrown into be made seven times hotter.

Again, in the book of Daniel we see another instance of "seven times" of punishment. God wanted to humble King Nebuchadnezzar of Babylon so He told him that he would become as a beast, eating grass with the cattle for a period of seven times.

> And you shall be driven from among men and your dwelling will be with the living creatures of the field. You will be made to eat grass like the oxen, and seven times [or years] shall pass over you until you have learned and know that the Most High [God] rules in the kingdom of men and gives it to whomever He will.
> Daniel 4:32 (AMP)

Nebuchadnezzar spent seven literal years living as a beast in fulfillment of the seven times prophecy. So a prophetic time is a period of one year.

Since Leviticus 26 is a prophecy, the "seven times" refers to seven prophetic "times". A prophetic, "time" is a 360 day prophetic year consisting of twelve 30 day months. This is because at creation the earth traveled around the sun in 360 days and the moon traveled around the earth in 30 days. This is evident in the days of Noah starting with Genesis 7:11. Noah and his family went into the ark on the 17th day of the second month. Then verse 24 says the waters covered the earth for 150 days. Next Genesis 8:4 tells us the ark came to rest on mount Ararat on the 17th day of the seventh month. Here is a period of 5 months and a period of 150 days, meaning that each month had exactly 30 days. You can find different theories which explain how that either the flood or some occurrence shortly thereafter caused the rotation of the earth to change so that the time it takes the moon to circle the earth is now 29.5 days and the earth travels around the sun in 365.25 days. The Hebrew calendar is a lunar calendar and has months alternating between 29 and 30 days. Some years have 12 months and some have 13 months in order to bring the beginning of the sacred year back to the spring equinox. So God uses a year of 360 days in order to calculate time prophetically.

During Israel's punishment, each day represented a year in fulfillment as shown in Numbers and Ezekiel.

> "According to the number of the days in which you spied out the land, forty days, **for each day you shall bear your guilt one year**, namely forty years, and you shall know My rejection."
> Numbers 14:34 Emphasis added.

> "Moreover take for yourself an iron plate, and set it as an iron wall between you and the city. Set your face against it, and it shall be besieged, and you shall lay siege against it. This will be **a sign to the *House of Israel*.** Lie also on your left side, and lay the iniquity of the *House of Israel* upon it. According to the number of the days that you lie on it, you shall bear their iniquity. **For I have laid on you the years of their iniquity, according to the number of the days, three hundred and ninety days; so you shall bear the iniquity of the *House of Israel*.** And when you have completed them, lie again on your right side; then you shall bear the iniquity of the *House of Judah* forty days. I have laid on you **a day for each year.**"
> Ezekiel 4:3-6 Emphasis added.

This "sign to the *House of Israel*" is telling them that their punishment will be one year for each day in the "seven times" punishment mentioned in Numbers 26.

To understand this key to prophetic timing we must study Revelation 12:6, 14, and 13:5. A thorough explanation of this can be found in Adam Clark's Commentary on Revelation 12:14. In brief, there are three values given: "A thousand two hundred and sixty days"; a "time, times, and half a time"; and "forty two months." These verses deal both with a past historic span of 1,260 years as well as a literal three and one half years yet to be fulfilled in the future, showing that God counts prophetic time like this:

- Each prophetic year has exactly 360 days
- Each prophetic month has thirty days
- Each prophetic day symbolizes one year in fulfillment.

The fact that forty two months, 1260 days, and three and one half years are all the same length of time is a key to understanding the "seven times" Israel would bear their iniquities being deprived of their national greatness and the great inheritance God promised to Ephraim and Manasseh in fulfillment of the birthright promises.

Now it becomes clear that the "seven times" of Leviticus 26:24 is speaking of seven years consisting of 360 days each. Therefore 7 x 360 days = 2,520 days. By applying the day for a year principle, each day then represents a year of national punishment for Israel, and a period of 2520 years the birthright blessing would be withheld.

The *House of Israel* ceased to be a kingdom in 718 B.C. when they started wandering northwest from their land to the British Isles. Subtracting 718 from 2520 because of the crossing over from B.C. to A.D. gives us 1802, and because there is no year zero, adding 1 to compensate for the lost year, we arrive at the year 1803.

Prior to 1800, Britain and the United States were relatively insignificant nations. Britain consisted of the British Isles, India and a few islands. Then in 1800, exactly 2520 years from the fall of Samaria, the capital city of the *House of Israel* to the Assyrians in 721 B.C., the capital of the United States moved from Philadelphia to Washington D.C.! From the arrival of the first colonists, through the forming of the United States, until 1803 the territory remained small being made up of the 13 original colony states and three additional states. Neither Britain nor the United States had great wealth or power. But 1803 was the year of the Louisiana Purchase which brought national wealth and power to the United States by adding multiplied hundreds of acres of land including over 500 million acres of the most fertile farmland in the world. This area became the "breadbasket of the world," and still exports much of its produce to feed other nations of the world just as Joseph in the days of famine provided food to the world. Truly, the United States has been a blessing to those nations who would receive it.

Every major sea gate in the world (such as Gibralter, Suez Canal, Hong Kong, Panama Canal, which was created by the United States) came under the possession or control of Britain and the United States.

The Industrial Revolution began in Britain in the 1750s, and by 1800 London was the financial and trading capital of the world. In 1803 Henry Maudslay created the first industrial assembly line using specialized machinery to manufacture rigging for the Royal Navy at Portsmouth, England. Britain, like a vine spreading over the wall, became a Company of Nations in the British Empire. Later the nations of the Commonwealth were given Dominion status by being made free and independent of England. They became a great Company or Commonwealth of Nations, joined not by a common government, but only by the head of state of all the Commonwealth, the Throne of David! This happened exactly "seven times" after the *House of Israel* ceased to exist in 718 B.C.!

Palestine Returns to the Jewish People After 2520 Years

Babylon ruled over the territory of the *House of Judah* from 604 B.C. starting with the captivity of Jehoiachin. Zedekiah the last king of the *House of Judah* was placed in that position as a vassal king and was to remain subject to Babylonian rule. Remember that in the 17th chapter of Ezekiel is a riddle and parable of the turning over of the crown from the *House of Judah* to the *House of Israel*. One of the main reasons given there for the throwing down of the throne in Jerusalem is given in Ezekiel 17:13-16:

"Then he took a member of the royal family and made a treaty with him, putting him under oath. He also carried away the leading men of the land, so that the kingdom would be brought low, unable to rise again, surviving only by keeping his treaty. But the king rebelled against him by sending his envoys to Egypt to get horses and a large army. Will he succeed? Will he who does such things escape? Will he break the treaty and yet escape? As surely as I live, declares the Sovereign LORD, he shall die in Babylon, in the land of the king who put him on the throne, whose oath he despised and whose treaty he broke."

Ezekiel 17:13-16 (NIV)

Zedekiah did not keep the treaty, or covenant, he had made to be subject to the king of Babylon, so his dynasty was terminated. This happened some seventeen years after Jehoiachin's captivity. But the real governor of Jerusalem was Nebuchadnezzar, not Zedekiah. Even after the Babylonians were overthrown by the Medes and Persians and a band of Jews were permitted to return to rebuild the walls of Jerusalem and to reestablish the temple in the days of Ezra and Nehemiah, there was no Jewish control of the city and of Palestine except as it came from the foreign capital.

If we apply the same one day for a year formula of "seven times" to the Jews losing their inheritance, we subtract 604 from 2520 to arrive at 1916 A.D.; we must then add a year because of the transition from 1 B.C. to 1 A.D. without a year zero in between, arriving at 1917 A.D.

On November 2, 1917 the British issued "The Balfour Declaration" in support of a Jewish homeland (see Appendix A) and preparing the way for the first Jewish immigrants to Palestine. The *House of Judah* got some of their land back, and finally in 1948, after the Second World War, they were granted full rights to establish the modern nation known to the world as Israel.

1917 is the same year General Allenby of the British Forces captured Gaza, Beersheba, and other places in Palestine, and entered Jerusalem on December 11ᵗʰ, exactly "seven times," after the conquest of the *House of Judah* by Babylon. The British, the modern descendants of Ephraim, along with troops from the Commonwealth Nations of Australia and New Zealand liberated Jerusalem from Turkey. A member of the royal line of David, now reigning from the *House of Israel* in Britain, again had governmental authority in Palestine and Jerusalem. In short, Jerusalem was no longer "trodden down of the Gentiles" (Luke 21:24). Perhaps much of Christianity is looking to the future for a prophetic event that has been and is being fulfilled beginning in 1917.

Chapter 14
What Have We Learned?

The main thing we have learned is that God is faithful to His word. When He says that he will bless the children of Israel, separating the Birthright promise from the Sceptre promise, He has a purpose. When He says that He will establish the throne of David and create a lasting dynasty ruling over the *House of Israel*, He will accomplish what He says. When He declares that you would have to stop the earth from turning and the stars from shining to keep Him from fulfilling His word, He means every word He says.

In short, God is not a liar (Romans 3:4). All the promises He made to Abraham, Isaac, Jacob and all the sons of Israel have not fallen to the ground without being fulfilled.

We have also learned that if you want to find the United States, the most powerful nation in the history of the world, in the Bible, you must not be looking for a "Gentile" people just because Americans do not look nor act like the Jews. Joseph, one of Israel's sons, married an Egyptian so his descendants would have ties to Egypt. Each of the twelve sons of Israel came from one of four mothers so they would naturally have different characteristics. Leah and Rachel were sisters, Jacob's cousins, the daughters of Laban, the brother of Jacob's mother Rebecca. Zilpah and Bilhah were slaves given to the two sisters as their father's wedding gifts.

Regarding the mothers of Israel's grandchildren, it seems significant that we know nothing of them except for Joseph's wife Asenath, an Egyptian, and Judah's wife Shuah, a Cannanite, the mother of Judah's three legitimate sons, two of whom died childless, and Judah's daughter-in-law Tamar through whom he begot the twins Perez and Zerah. These mothers of Israel's grandchildren are significant because through them came the possessors of the birthright and of the sceptre promises.

Genesis Scripture	Jacob's Wives and Concubines and Their Children (See Appendix B)				Name Meaning
	Leah	Bilhah	Zilpah	Rachel	
29:32	Reuben				See, a son
29:33	Simeon				Heard
29:34	Levi				Attached
29:35	Judah				Praise
30:6		Dan			Judge
30:8		Naphtali			My Wrestling
30:11			Gad		Troop or Fortune
30:13			Asher		Happy
30:18	Issachar				Hire
30:20	Zebulun				Dwelling
30:24				Joseph	He Will Add
35:18				Benjamin	Son of the Right Hand

In addition, we have seen that the birthright blessings, which were withheld for 2520 years began to be bestowed upon Britain and the United States right on schedule in the early years of the 19th century. In addition, a member of the royal family of David took governmental oversight of Palestine, preparing the way for the establishing of the Jewish nation called Israel exactly 2520 years after Jehoiachin was the last king of David's dynasty to hold sovereign rule in Jerusalem.

Finally, we have come to understand that there is a difference between the *House of Israel* and the *House of Judah* when we look at the Bible and prophecy. Many who don't understand this difference see only the small nation called Israel in the Middle East whenever they see prophecy, however, many prophecies commonly attributed to the Jews are actually about the *House of Israel.*

For example, the book of Ezekiel is primarily written to the *House of Israel*, and sometimes to the Jews. Many current prophecy preachers and teachers are looking for things to happen in the Middle East because of their misreading of this book. Let's review a very popular prophecy that is used to show the return of the Jews to Palestine. It is found in the 34th chapter of Ezekiel. The prophecy starts out with a valley of dry bones, which most interpret to be the Jews, but verse 11 says:

> Then He said to me, "Son of man, these bones are the whole *House of Israel.* They indeed say, 'Our bones are dry, our hope is lost, and we ourselves are cut off!'"
> Ezekiel 37:11

The very scripture they say refers to the Jews, or the *House of Judah*, specifically says the bones are the "whole *House of Israel*," the same people much of the book of Ezekiel is about. At the time this was written, the *House of Israel* had been taken captive by the Assyrians, and the *House of Judah* was about to go into captivity at the hands of the Babylonians. The *House of Israel* had lost hope and had been cut off. They were as if dead. This event is described before the next section of the chapter in which there is a restoration of the relationship between the *House of Israel* and the *House of Judah* in verses 15 and following.

Ezekiel chapters 38 and 39 are often called the battle of Gog and Magog against the Jewish state in the land of Palestine. However, notice what we read in chapter 39:

> "And you, son of man, prophesy against Gog, and say, 'Thus says the Lord God: "Behold, I am against you, O Gog, the prince of Rosh, Meshech, and Tubal; and I will turn you around and lead you on, bringing you up from the far north, and

bring you against **the mountains of Israel**. Then I will knock the bow out of your left hand, and cause the arrows to fall out of your right hand. You shall fall upon **the mountains of Israel**, you and all your troops and the peoples who are with you; I will give you to birds of prey of every sort and to the beasts of the field to be devoured.'"
Ezekiel 39:1-4 Emphasis added.

The term "mountains of Israel" refers to the region of the original home of the entire nation Israel, so these scriptures apparently refer to that region. Prophecy teachers tell us that as a result of this war the Jews will be cleaning up dead bodies for seven months following the defeat of Gog and Magog, but read what Ezekiel actually wrote:

For seven months the *House of Israel* will be burying them, in order to cleanse the land.
Ezekiel 39:12 Emphasis added.

"I will set My glory among the nations; all the nations shall see My judgment which I have executed, and My hand which I have laid on them. So **the *House of Israel*** shall know that I am the Lord their God from that day forward. The Gentiles shall know that **the *House of Israel*** went into captivity for their iniquity; because they were unfaithful to Me, therefore I hid My face from them. I gave them into the hand of their enemies, and they all fell by the sword. According to their uncleanness and according to their transgressions I have dealt with them, and hidden My face from them."
Ezekiel 39:21-24 Emphasis added.

These illustrations only show that we can misinterpret the prophecies of the Bible and apply them to the wrong people if we aren't aware that the Jews are not the *House of Israel*, and the *House of Israel* didn't return to Palestine when the Jews returned. The first time the Jews returned during the days of Ezra and Nehemiah, the *House of Israel* was being sifted through all nations and many of them would eventually settle in the British Isles and other parts of Europe. The *House of Israel* had already settled in their new homelands when the Jews returned following the Second World War. In fact, if it hadn't been for the *House of Israel*, the homeland the Jews now enjoy would not have been given to them.

What about the Jews?

> What advantage then has the Jew, or what is the profit of circumcision? Much in every way! Chiefly because to them were committed the oracles of God. For what if some did not believe? Will their unbelief make the faithfulness of God without effect?
> Romans 3:1-3

The question naturally comes up, "Does this teaching do harm to the Christian understanding of the Jewish people?" to which I say, "In no way!" God is beginning to bring a fresh revelation of the importance of the Jewish people to the ongoing life of the church. After all, the apostle Paul tells us in Romans 3:2, "to them were committed the oracles of God." What does that mean? Simply that God committed the writings of the Old Testament as well as many of the "traditions," or extra-biblical writings to the Jewish people, who include the tribe of Benjamin and much of the tribe of Levi, the priestly tribe. Anyone who has studied the extra-biblical writings of the Jewish people knows that there are some things which the New Testament shows were completely wrong in their understanding of God. However, there is a lot

Christians can learn from the Jews to better understand the roots of our faith and God's purposes for His children.

It was to the Jews God gave the responsibility of creating and preserving the cannon of the Old Testament scriptures, and we rely on them for that. In fact, if the Jews had not kept the sacred writings we would have no idea where to look for the lost tribes of Israel, or even that there are other Israelite nations besides the Jews in the middle east nation called Israel.

Chapter 15
Conclusion or
Why Is it Important?

As mentioned in the Preface there are those who believe it is not necessary to understand the Israelite history of Britain and The United States, as affecting a person's salvation, and they are absolutely right. Salvation is a result of faith in the sacrifice of Jesus Christ upon the cross and in his resurrection. **Period**.

> But what does it say? "The word is near you, in your mouth and in your heart" (that is, the word of faith which we preach): that **if you confess with your mouth the Lord Jesus and believe in your heart that God has raised Him from the dead, you will be saved.** For with the heart one believes unto righteousness, and with the mouth confession is made unto salvation.
> Romans 10:8-10 Emphasis added.

However, as the author of "The Covenant People" explains on pages 82 - 85, if a person came to you saying they had discovered that they were the heir of vast estates, great wealth, power and responsibility, but instead of rejoicing and receiving the wealth in order to fulfill the responsibility they said something like "it really doesn't matter" you might question their reasoning and/or willingness to accept responsibility. Some Christians, upon learning these truths might say, "I have Jesus and that is all I need; being an Israelite won't save my soul." But these same Christians upon learning of a will making them heir of a fortune, granting them lands, wealth, position, responsibility and privilege would not say, "What if I am; that won't save my soul." Rather, if they were truly a Christian would accept the inheritance and use all in their power to bless and help the world, fulfilling the commission Jesus gave to preach the gospel in all the world.

Those who see salvation as the only message of the Bible often believe that the church is all there is of Israel today and want to ignore the national promises and prophesies of the Old Testament as if they were irrelevant to the church today. These are the same people who refuse to believe that the return of the Jews to Palestine has any significance because they want to see all prophecy as being fulfilled in the past or by the church. That would be convenient, but it just isn't the case.

While I don't particularly believe that everything prophecy teachers say is Biblical, it is true that world events are moving toward the conclusion of the age, preparing for the coming of the Lord Jesus Christ in all His glory to reign over the earth. Most of those who are in the former category seem to believe that when the Lord returns, we will all go to heaven and live there for eternity, that the saints will not reign on earth. When each presents their point of view, it can be easy to believe, until the whole thing is reviewed in light of all scripture. The subject of God's purpose for creating mankind and the plan He is working out must be left for another book.

Why would God create a nation and promise it national greatness by seemingly unbreakable promises, and then irrevocably cast off that nation once they sinned and received their punishment? Romans 11:29, speaking of all Israel, not just the Jews, says "For the gifts and the calling of God are irrevocable." Either God is going to keep His word, or He is not. If not, then what part of the Bible can we believe? Part of the answer to this is wrapped up in understanding the purpose of Israel, both the *House of Israel*, and the *House of Judah*. The gifts and the calling of God go together! The gifts are given in order to fulfill the calling.

America's Founding Fathers believed that The United States was guided and established by Divine Providence to be an example and a blessing to the entire human race. They believed in a sense of mission and responsibility rather than "racial superiority." The former is a call to leadership and service while the latter is nothing more than the arrogant presumption of a self-appointed role to conquer and rule.

While the Constitution was being prepared, John Adams wrote the following from England:

> "The people of America have now the best opportunity and the greatest trust in their hands that Providence ever committed to so small a number." (Koch, *The American Enlightenment*, p 257 as quoted in *The 5000 Year Leap*)

If we, the people of the United States of America and Britain are the rightful holders of the birthright blessings promised to Abraham, Isaac, and Jacob, we must take heed that we do not fall into the sin of Esau.

> lest there be any fornicator or profane person like Esau, who **for one morsel of food sold his birthright**. For you know that afterward, when he wanted to inherit the blessing, he was rejected, for he found no place for repentance, though he sought it diligently with tears.
> Hebrews 12:16-17 Emphasis added.

I am concerned that we as a people are giving away our birthright for something that will prove to be worthless in the end. Then when we have lost it, we will find it is very hard to retrieve.

God did not choose the sons of Abraham, Isaac, and Jacob to receive special treatment. He chose them because He needed an example in the earth to all the nations of the blessings that come upon any nation whose God is the Lord! (Psalm 33:12) Notice what Moses said to Israel before they went into the promised land:

> Surely I have taught you statutes and judgments, just as the Lord my God commanded me, that you

should act according to them in the land which you go to possess. Therefore be careful to observe them; **for this is your wisdom and your understanding in the sight of the peoples** who will hear all these statutes, and say, 'Surely this great nation is a wise and understanding people.' For what great nation is there that has God so near to it, as the Lord our God is to us, for whatever reason we may call upon Him? And what great nation is there that has such statutes and righteous judgments as are in all this law which I set before you this day?
Deuteronomy 4:5-8 Emphasis added.

God chose Israel to be the nation through which Jesus would be born in order to provide the way of salvation for all mankind. He also chose Israel to be the nation who would follow His ways and show the blessings obedience would bring the nations of the earth who, for the most part, have been living in idolatry from the tower of Babel until now!

When the Most High divided their inheritance to the nations, When He separated the sons of Adam, He set the boundaries of the peoples according to the number of the children of Israel. For the Lord's portion is His people; Jacob is the place of His inheritance.
Deuteronomy 32:8-9

Once the *House of Israel* was removed from their original land, they were moved, sifted through the nations until they came to the new homeland God had prepared according to their number when He divided the nations and gave them their inheritances. The *House of Israel* was also prepared to receive the Gospel which their brother nation, the *House of Judah*, had, for the most part, rejected. Jesus, knowing that the Jews were going to reject Him said,

> "I was not sent except to the lost sheep of **the House of Israel**."
> Matthew 15:24 Emphasis added.

To the chief priests and elders of the Jews Jesus also said:

> "Therefore I say to you, the kingdom of God will be taken from you and given to a nation bearing the fruits of it."
> Matthew 21:43

And to His disciples, he said,

> These twelve Jesus sent out and commanded them, saying: "Do not go into the way of the Gentiles, and do not enter a city of the Samaritans. But **go rather to the lost sheep of the *House of Israel*."**
> Matthew 10:5-6 Emphasis added.

Evidence exists that shows the original apostles, except those who were martyred in or around Jerusalem, went out seeking the *House of Israel* where they found a much more receptive audience than among the Jews of Judea. The original twelve never went except to Israelites, either of the *House of Judah*, or of the *House of Israel*.

Paul's calling was a little different. Read what the Lord told Ananias when he protested against giving help to Saul after his Damascus road experience.

> But the Lord said to him, "Go, for he is a chosen vessel of Mine to bear My name before Gentiles, kings, and the children of Israel. For I will show

him how many things he must suffer for My name's sake."
Acts 9:15-16

Paul's primary calling was to the nations (Gentiles) and kings, and later to the children of Israel. All of the original apostles preached exclusively to either the *House of Israel* or to the Jews. They were told that once they were scattered from Jerusalem, they would

> "But you shall receive power when the Holy Spirit has come upon you; and you shall be witnesses to Me in **Jerusalem**, and in **all Judea** and **Samaria**, and **to the end of the earth**."
> Acts 1:8

Shortly after the *House of Israel* was removed from the Promised Land, Hosea was given the following message for them when his son was born:

> Then God said: "Call his name Lo-Ammi, for you are not My people, and I will not be your God. Yet the number of the children of Israel shall be as the sand of the sea, which cannot be measured or numbered. And it shall come to pass in the place where it was said to them, 'You are not My people,' there it shall be said to them, 'You are sons of the living God.'"
> Hosea 1:9-10

The message of salvation which was brought to the *House of Israel* took root and has borne much fruit, so much so that until recent years the British and Americans have sent out the majority of missionaries to the nations. The United States was founded on Christian principles, and has used those principles, along with the British, to become the most charitable people on the earth, providing assistance to nations everywhere, fulfilling the promise that through Israel all other nations of the earth would be blessed. The *House of Judah* has blessed the world by the fulfillment of the promise of the savior and the *House of Israel* has blessed the world materially just like their forefather Joseph did so long ago. Joseph's descendants, the possessors of the physical birthright blessing, provides material blessing to the world, while Judah's descendants, the possessors of the sceptre promise provided the blessing of salvation for the world through their Messiah who most of them have rejected. The *House of Israel* has also used the material blessings as a means of proclaiming the good news of the Messiah to the world. However, I believe the fullness of the responsibility God gave the House of Israel has not yet been completed.

And yet, there is another reason the identity of the United States is important, the covenants.

Chapter 16
America's Covenants with God

God made several covenants with the Patriarchs as mentioned in previous chapters. These covenants came with promises of future greatness. These covenants were discussed in regard to Abraham, Isaac, Jacob/Israel and King David. However, when we consider the United States in prophecy we must understand how God looks at specific covenants between our people and the God of Israel. Let us first start by looking at the period of the founding of the United States.

There is controversy among people today as to whether or not the founders had a covenant with God. Those who say there is no covenant are primarily those who deny the Christian influence on the Founders. They are in denial and refuse to look at the actual history of the time. Those who say there is a Christian covenant between the United States and God do so based upon several documents.

There are four documents which form the basis of the United States of America. Most people consider the Constitution, and some the Declaration of Independence, but there are two more documents that are at the very heart of out great republic. All of our founding documents are these:

- Mayflower Compact - November 11, 1620
- Articles of Confederation of the United Colonies of New England - May 19, 1643
- The Declaration of Independence - July 4, 1776
- The Constitution of the United States - September 17, 1787

The Mayflower Compact contains these words, "In the Name of God, Amen. We whose names are underwritten . . . having undertaken for the glory of God and the advancement of the Christian faith, a voyage to plant the first colony . . . do by these

Presents, solemnly and mutually, in the presence of God, combine ourselves into a civil body politic." *This is the beginning of our politics.*

The Articles of Confederation of the United Colonies of New England were written by a man of God to join the first four colonies **into one people.** *It was the forerunner of our government* and states, "Whereas we all came into these parts of America with one and the same end and aim, namely, to advance the Kingdom of our Lord Jesus Christ and to enjoy the liberties of the Gospel in purity with peace. . . We therefore do conceive it our bounder duty. . . That, as in nation and religion, so in other respects, we be and continue one."

The Declaration of Independence contains these words starting in the second paragraph, "We hold these truths to be self-evident, that all men are created equal, that they are endowed by their Creator with certain unalienable rights, that among these are life, liberty and the pursuit of happiness. That to secure these rights, governments are instituted among men, deriving their just powers from the consent of the governed." *This Declaration made us a nation.*

Each of these three documents have reference to God and two of them declare openly that the purpose of our forefathers in coming to this continent was to establish a Christian nation, with a Christian purpose, to bless the whole world. These three documents are not open to amendment or change.

The Constitution of the United States begins with these words, "We the People of the United States, . . . do ordain and establish this Constitution for the United States of America." *The Constitution is the blueprint for our administrative political machinery,* and although it does not mention God directly it is bound to the other three documents that preceded it. Notice that it is "We the People" who established these documents and the institutions created by them.

I will leave it for you to decide if you believe the Founders entered into a covenant with God. Remember that although there were people from Spain and France who claimed part of the continent, it was the people who came from Britain who are responsible for the form of government we enjoy. Also remember that in chapter 11 we studied the Hebrew Names of Britain, and that when you look at the Hebrew meaning of the word Brit-ish we find they are the Covenant People, implying that there was a covenant existing prior to the Mayflower Compact. Let's look at that covenant because it will reveal a lot about the United States as well as the British Commonwealth.

We have already identified the British and American people as the tribes of Joseph, Ephraim and Manasseh. These tribes were present when God established the tribes of Israel into a nation at Mount Sinai. These events are recorded in Exodus chapters 19 to 24.

After being freed from Egyptian bondage the Israelites came to the wilderness of Sinai and in Exodus the 19th chapter, God spoke to Moses and began the process of establishing this covenant. Notice the following:

> And Moses went up to God, and the Lord called to him from the mountain, saying, "Thus you shall say to the house of Jacob, and tell the children of Israel: 'You have seen what I did to the Egyptians, and how I bore you on eagles' wings and brought you to Myself. Now therefore, if you will indeed obey My voice and keep My covenant, then you shall be a special treasure to Me above all people; for all the earth is Mine. And you shall be to Me a kingdom of priests and a holy nation.' These are the words which you shall speak to the children of Israel." So Moses came and called for the elders of the people, and laid before them all these words which the Lord commanded him. Then all the people answered together and said, "All that the Lord has spoken we will do." So Moses brought back the words of the people to the Lord.
> Exodus 19:3-8

Moses was instructed to have the people consecrate themselves for three days in preparation for the next step in the covenant-making process. In the 20th chapter of Exodus God spoke the Ten Commandments to all the people. They were so frightened by the sound of God's voice they told Moses, "You speak with us, and we will hear; but let not God speak with us, lest we die." (Exodus 20:18-19) One of the things God wanted for them was to be a people who heard God individually for themselves, but that is a subject for another time and place.

There were several parts to the covenant God made with Israel here in Exodus chapters 19 through 23. These included the following:

- The Ten Commandments - Exodus 20:1-17
- Various civil laws and judgments - Exodus 21:1-23:9
- The Sabbath - Exodus 23:10-13
- Annual Feasts - Exodus 23:14-19

Then at the conclusion of these things, God called Moses and seventy of the elders of the people to the mountain, the elders stayed some distance away, while God and Moses talked face to face regarding the sealing of the covenant.

> So Moses came and told the people all the words of the Lord and all the judgments. And all the people answered with one voice and said, "All the words which the Lord has said we will do."
> Exodus 24:3

Notice that it wasn't just the elders, the leaders of the people agreeing to enter into this covenant, but "all the people answered with one voice." In other words it was an act of "We the People" entering into this covenant. In Exodus 24:4-6 preparation was made for a special ceremony of "cutting the covenant" and sealing it with blood. God was serious about the significance of what was going on here.

> Then he took the Book of the Covenant and read
> in the hearing of the people. And they said, "All
> that the Lord has said we will do, and be
> obedient."
> Exodus 24:7

This was the final statement required to seal the covenant and obligate God to do His part and the people to do their part. A short time later, God called Moses to the mountain to receive the Ten Commandments on tablets of stone and to receive instructions regarding the Tabernacle. During this time the people turned from God and entered into idolatry, and Moses broke the tablets. God called Moses again to the mountain, and again wrote out the commandments. Notice what Moses says next:

> And the Lord said to Moses, "Cut two tablets of
> stone like the first ones, and I will write on these
> tablets the words that were on the first tablets
> which you broke." So he was there with the Lord
> forty days and forty nights; he neither ate bread
> nor drank water. And He wrote on the tablets the
> words of the covenant, the Ten Commandments.
> Exodus 34:1,28

The important thing here is that the words of the covenant consisted of the Ten Commandments. All the other statutes, judgments and laws of this covenant were established upon the foundation of the Ten Commandments. Prior to the death of Moses he reminded the people of their history and of the covenant they'd entered into. Notice what he said:

> So He declared to you His covenant which He
> commanded you to perform, the Ten
> Commandments; and He wrote them on two
> tablets of stone.
> Deuteronomy 4:13

If you will study the history of the founding of the United States, you will find that this basic law of God was used as a foundation for our civil government along with the rest of the Bible. It is also significant that now the Ten Commandments are being removed from prominent places in our society.

I have taken a long time to explain the covenant between God and Israel. But, you might ask, what does that have to do with us? Good question! If what you have read to this point leads you to the conclusion that the United States is composed of descendants of Joseph and his eldest son Manasseh, it becomes very significant because our forefathers were there when this covenant was made. But, you might also ask, doesn't that just apply to them, and not to us? See what Moses said:

> God, our God, made a covenant with us at Horeb.
> God didn't just make this covenant with our
> parents; he made it also with us, with all of us
> who are alive right now.
> Deuteronomy 5:2-3 (MSG)

You might still say, well that was them and we're not bound by what they did about four thousand years ago. Well, read a New Testament scripture which sheds light on this subject.

> Even Levi, who receives tithes, paid tithes through
> Abraham, so to speak, for he was still in the loins
> of his father when Melchizedek met him.
> Hebrews 7:9-10

What the writer of Hebrews is saying is that what was done by Abraham was accounted by God to have been done by Levi his great-grandson and all of Levi's children who received tithes even in the days of Jesus and later when there was still a temple in Jerusalem. Do you suppose that after the deportation of the northern *House of Israel* by Assyria in 718 B.C. God decided the covenant no longer applied to their descendants when the reason

God allowed them to be deported was the breaking of this covenant, especially as it concerns the second commandment regarding idolatry, the breaking of the Sabbaths and the violation of most of the civil statutes and laws? I think not!

If we look into the future, during what is called the Millennium, we see the tribes of Israel being the premier nations, leading the way to God. This will be led by the Sceptre holders of Judah, and the Birthright people of Joseph, Britain and the United States.

> So Jesus said to them, "Assuredly I say to you, that in the regeneration, when the Son of Man sits on the throne of His glory, you who have followed Me will also sit on twelve thrones, judging the twelve tribes of Israel."
> Matthew 19:28

> And I bestow upon you a kingdom, just as My Father bestowed one upon Me, that you may eat and drink at My table in My kingdom, and sit on thrones judging the twelve tribes of Israel.
> Luke 22:29-30

Each of the disciples of Jesus will sit on a throne, ruling one of the twelve tribes under the King of Kings, Jesus, who will rule from Jerusalem upon the throne of David, which is currently held by Queen Elizabeth of Britain.

Covenants have consequences. There are two places in the books of Moses, Leviticus chapter 26 and Deuteronomy chapter 28, which describe the blessings for obedience to the covenant and the curses for disobedience. Others who speak of the United States and the things that are happening now and are likely to happen in the future quote these two chapters, yet they almost universally refuse to admit what I think they know in their hearts, that if the United States isn't a part of natural Israel, they can't be under this covenant. Yet, as we shall see in the next chapter, many things that are prophesied to come upon Israel for breaking this covenant are happening to the people of Britain, the United States, and western Europe, but not to other nations such as India, China, the Islamic nations, etc. They have their own issues, but no one connects them back to the covenants with Israel because they are not included.

Chapter 17
What about the Future?

There was a time when I thought I had the end times all figured out. I have since become more cautious in making dogmatic statements of what I believe the future holds. However, there are some very interesting things happening today, which appear to be the beginning of fulfilling some Bible prophecies.

> But if you do not obey Me, and do not observe all these commandments, and if you despise My statutes, or if your soul abhors My judgments, so that you do not perform all My commandments, but break My covenant, I also will do this to you: **I will even appoint terror over you**, wasting disease and fever which shall consume the eyes and cause sorrow of heart. And you shall sow your seed in vain, for your enemies shall eat it.
> Leviticus 26:14-16 Emphasis added.

On September 11, 2001 I was working at my desk and considering the horror which had just occurred when I realized that several things had happened. The United States had been in a war of terror for several years, although failing to recognize it as such and to call it that. Airplanes were used in an attempt to destroy the might of our great country. The World Trade Center in New York represented the economic power of the United States, while the Pentagon represents the military power of the United States. Two airplanes took down the towers of the World Trade Center while a third plane hit the Pentagon. A fourth airplane may have been headed for the nation's capital in an attempt to destroy the governmental power of The United States. This day initiated what later came to be called the "War on Terror," a war most people do not understand and some think doesn't exist. Prior to 9/11 we had been struck by terrorists in an attempt to destroy one of the twin towers, by attacks on our embassies, our military barracks, and by attacking the USS Cole, just to name a few. While the United States has maintained some semblance of devotion to God, His hand of protection has been upon us. However, the more we have tried to remove God from our public recognition, God has been forced to remove His hand of protection. We kick God out of the schools, the judicial branch of government, etc. then we wonder why He isn't there to protect us when we need Him. It seems that as a people we have forgotten the history of how we became such a great people. Rather, there has been a concerted effort in our educational system to remove that knowledge from us.

Another thing which came to mind that day in September 2001 is this verse:

I will break the pride of your power.
Leviticus 26:19 Emphasis added

The attacks that day were against the major strengths and powers of the United States; Economic, Military, and Governmental. Depending on the type of government we have in place at any one time, our pride in the power God has granted to us has been eroding and in some cases it seems to be despised. There is attack after attack against our military might even within the houses of congress and the White House. It is as though we have become ashamed of the gift God has given us for good and are willing to back down in the face of smaller nations. We are more concerned about our "image" before the world than our image before God.

> I will set My face against you, and **you shall be defeated by your enemies**. Those who hate you shall reign over you, and **you shall flee when no one pursues you**.
> Leviticus 26:17 Emphasis added.

Until the Korean and Vietnam Wars the United States was undefeated. Now it seems that much of the time we're willing to back down when no one in the world is chasing us. The pride of our power is being broken.

Read the 28th chapter of Deuteronomy and you will see a chronicle of the blessings of God on the British and American people over the last two centuries. Notice just a few things that are mentioned.

> Now it shall come to pass, if you diligently obey the voice of the Lord your God, to observe carefully all His commandments which I command you today, that **the Lord your God will set you high above all nations of the earth**. And all these blessings shall come upon you and overtake you, because you obey the voice of the Lord your God: Blessed shall you be in the city, and blessed shall you be in the country. Blessed shall be the fruit of your body, the produce of your ground and the increase of your herds, the increase of your cattle and the offspring of your flocks. Blessed shall be your basket and your kneading bowl.
>
> Deuteronomy 28:1-5 Emphasis added.

These promises have never been fulfilled in any other nation that has ever existed to the degree they have in our time. True, there have been several world-ruling empires in the past: Egypt; Assyria; Babylon; Media-Persia; Greece; Rome. God wasn't speaking to any of these non-Israelite nations, but to the nations of Israel. This promise has not been fulfilled in the Jewish portion of Israel because they don't hold the birthright promise, which belongs exclusively to the tribes of Ephraim and Manasseh. But look further.

> The Lord will cause your enemies who rise
> against you to be defeated before your face; they
> shall come out against you one way and flee
> before you seven ways. . . Then all peoples of the
> earth shall see that you are called by the name of
> the Lord, and they shall be afraid of you.
> Deuteronomy 28:7, 10

It is because of the name of the Lord that the other nations of the world are afraid of the *House of Israel*. Remember the words of Jesus.

> Then they will deliver you up to tribulation and
> kill you, and you will be hated by all nations for
> My name's sake.
> Matthew 24:9

I am reminded of an incident that captured the news for several days in November 2008. Terrorists captured several buildings in Mumbai (Bombay), India and held Jews, Britons and Americans hostage before killing all the Jews and torturing the Britons and Americans. Radical Islam calls the Jewish nation "the little Satan" and the United States "the great Satan." As the focus of world attention is more and more on the Jewish state of Israel and the tension in the Middle East, it is imperative upon the brothers of the Jewish nation of Israel, Ephraim and Manasseh, Britain and the United States, to use the influence God has given them to stand with the Jews. When we have not stood with the small nation of Israel, there have been severe consequences that are seemingly out of proportion to what other nations experience.

Read another portion of Deuteronomy chapter 28.

> The alien who is among you shall rise higher and
> higher above you, and you shall come down lower
> and lower. He shall lend to you, but you shall not

lend to him; he shall be the head, and you shall be
the tail.
Deuteronomy 28:43-44

While the United States has always allowed and welcomed
immigration, the current situation with illegal immigration has the
potential to completely destroy the fabric of our society. In years
past, the United States was considered the "melting pot" where
immigrants came to take advantage of and become part of
American culture and the American way of life. Now we are
becoming a multi-cultural society. Many people crossing the
border from Mexico into America illegally don't want to be
Americans, they want to maintain their own separateness and
even want to overthrow the government. This is also true of some
Muslims who have an agenda to bring Islamic Sharia law to the
United States. They don't come here because they love America
and the opportunities they find as a result of our Christian
heritage, but because they have an agenda to rule the world their
way.

Also notice that God says that while we are under His
blessings, we would be lenders to the nations, but when we walk
away from Him and stop acknowledging Him as the source of our
greatness, we would become slaves to nations and people who
would lend to us. What do we see now? The government of the
United States is in the process of borrowing more money than the
nation can possibly pay back and at the same time changing the
whole foundation of our society. Remember the words of
Solomon.

The rich rules over the poor, And the borrower is
servant to the lender.
Proverbs 22:7

We are in the process or have already become a servant nation,
though not in the way God intended. Does this mean God cannot

or will not use His people in the future? He is still working out His own plan, and things may get worse before they get better.

> The Lord will strike you with **madness** and **blindness** and **confusion (astonishment - KJV) of heart**. And you shall grope at noonday, as a blind man gropes in darkness; you shall not prosper in your ways; you shall be only oppressed and plundered continually, and no one shall save you.
> Deuteronomy 28:28-29 Emphasis added.

Read Adam Clarke's Commentary on verse 28:

> **The Lord shall smite thee with madness**— וְעִגָּשׁ shiggaon, distraction, so that thou shalt not know what to do.
>
> **And blindness**— וְרוֹעֵ ivvaron, blindness, both physical and mental; the בָרג garab, (verse 27), destroying their eyes, and the judgments of God confounding their understandings.
>
> **Astonishment**— וְהִמַת timmahon, stupidity and amazement. By the just judgments of God they were so completely confounded, as not to discern the means by which they might prevent or remove their calamities, and to adopt those which led directly to their ruin.
>
> — Adam Clarke's Commentary

This sounds like the condition much of the United States and Britain find themselves in. While many propose solutions to our current problems, these solutions are often distractions from the course of action we should follow. In many ways we seem to be blind, that is confounded in our understanding because as a nation we have taken God out of much of our public discourse and thought. The result is that we are doing stupid things and many in our nation are full of amazement and dumfounded at what is happening. Sometimes we are so full of fear and confusion that we cannot discern the way to prevent or remove our calamities so we do things that only exacerbate our situation.

We must pray for our nation; first for His spiritual children to once again have a positive influence in their society; second for His natural children through Abraham, Isaac, Jacob, and all the tribes of Israel.

> If My people who are called by My name will humble themselves, and pray and seek My face, and turn from their wicked ways, then I will hear from heaven, and will forgive their sin and heal their land.
> 2 Chronicles 7:14

Prayer is very important, but as Christians we must begin to live our lives according to God's will which will produce a change in the outcomes for ourselves and set the example of righteousness for our brothers and sisters in the flesh. As Deuteronomy 4:6 tells us, the commandments and statutes of God are our wisdom in all areas of life.

At one time, I thought the United States and Britain, the primary nations of the *House of Israel*, were destined for a time of captivity and scattering as had previously happened to their ancestors and to the Jews. However, I am not so sure anymore. In spite of the move away from the founding principles of our nation, there is still a significant group of people who love God and want to see things change. The change can't be back to the way things were. God wants real change in the heart and soul of the British and American people. Obedience to God is the only way out of our current downward slide. In addition, I believe there is still a great responsibility placed upon the United States and Britain that has never been completely fulfilled. Perhaps the current circumstances are primarily intended by God to awaken His people and prepare them to lead the way out of the spiritual Egypt we find ourselves in.

So, who are the United States and Britain? Are they spoken of in Bible prophecy? If they are, "So what?" That is the question. In the end, time will tell.

> Surely the Lord God does nothing, unless He reveals His secret to His servants the prophets.
> Amos 3:7

Thank you for joining me on this journey through the prophetic word of God and history. You will have to decide for yourself if you believe this journey has been profitable.

Appendix A
The Balfour Declaration
November 2, 1917

During the First World War, British policy became gradually committed to the idea of establishing a Jewish home in Palestine (Eretz Yisrael). After discussions in the British Cabinet, and consultation with Zionist leaders, the decision was made known in the form of a letter by Arthur James Lord Balfour to Lord Rothschild. The letter represents the first political recognition of Zionist aims by a Great Power.

Foreign Office
November 2nd, 1917

Dear Lord Rothschild,

I have much pleasure in conveying to you, on behalf of His Majesty's Government, the following declaration of sympathy with Jewish Zionist aspirations which has been submitted to, and approved by, the Cabinet.

"His Majesty's Government view with favour the establishment in Palestine of a national home for the Jewish people, and will use their best endeavours to facilitate the achievement of this object, it being clearly understood that nothing shall be done which may prejudice the civil and religious rights of existing non-Jewish communities in Palestine, or the rights and political status enjoyed by Jews in any other country."

I should be grateful if you would bring this declaration to the knowledge of the Zionist Federation.

Yours sincerely,
Arthur James Balfour
Source: Israel Ministry of Foreign Affairs web site www.mfa.gov.i

Appendix B

Abraham's Family Tree

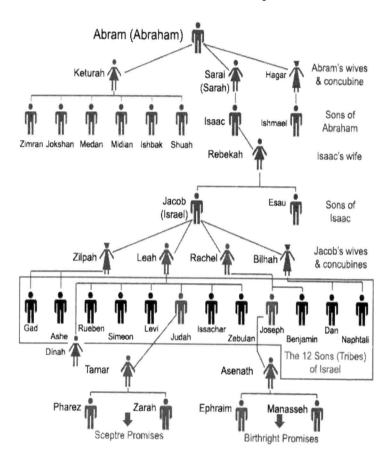

Taken from *"The U.S.A. & The British Commonwealth in Bible Prophecy"*
by Peter Salemi.
Used by permission. www.british-israel.ca

Appendix C
The Tribes

Ephraim – The British Commonwealth
Manasseh – The United States of America
Reuben – Northern France
Levi – Scattered, mostly with the Jews
Issachar – Finland
Zebulon – Holland
Benjamin – Iceland, Belgae, Normans, Quebecois
Dan – Danes, Irish
Napthali – Sweden
Yehuda – Jews - Tribe of Judah, Modern Israel and Scattered
Gad – Norway
Asher – Swiss
Simeon – Welsh

Taken from "*The U.S.A. & The British Commonwealth in Bible Prophecy*" by Peter Salemi. Used by permission.
www.british-israel.ca

Appendix D
The British Royal Coat of Arms

In Numbers 2:2-34 God instructed the tribes of Israel to divide into four groups of three tribes each when they set up camp, each group would arrange on one side of the square camp. Each group of tribes assembled behind the "standard" of the leading tribe on its side. The four lead tribes were Judah, Reuben, Ephraim and Dan. The ancient heraldic symbol on Ephraim's standard was a bull or ox, Dan's was an eagle, Reuben's was a man, and Judah's symbol was a lion.

There are several different ways the Royal Coat of Arms of the United Kingdom is presented. However, there are several items that are always present and which point us back to the *House of Israel*, and specifically to the tribe of Ephraim.

- The Lion on the left side is the tribal symbol of the tribe of Judah, the possessor of the sceptre promise. Remember that the royal line of David is from the tribe of Judah. In Genesis 49:9, Jacob said "Judah is a lion's whelp."
- The harp in the center shield is a symbol of king David, the Psalmist of Israel.
- The unicorn on the right side of the Coat of Arms is the symbol of Ephraim. When you read Deuteronomy 33:17 in the King James version, the word "unicorns" appears where in the New King James Version and other later versions the words "wild ox" appear. This is in reference to the tribe of Joseph, which is represented by Ephraim, the possessor of the birthright given to Joseph.
- Between the Lion and the Unicorn are the Old French words, *Hoi soit qui man y pense*, which mean "Evil to him who thinks evil" – of Britain, that is. Remember the promise of the birthright , "Cursed be everyone who curses you" (Genesis 27:29; cf. Numbers 24:9).

Appendix E
Matthias the Apostle

And when they had entered, they went up into the upper room where they were staying: Peter, James, John, and Andrew; Philip and Thomas; Bartholomew and Matthew; James the son of Alphaeus and Simon the Zealot; and Judas the son of James.

These all continued with one accord in prayer and supplication, with the women and Mary the mother of Jesus, and with His brothers. And in those days Peter stood up in the midst of the disciples (altogether the number of names was about a hundred and twenty), and said, "Men and brethren, this Scripture had to be fulfilled, which the Holy Spirit spoke before by the mouth of David concerning Judas, who became a guide to those who arrested Jesus; for he was numbered with us and obtained a part in this ministry." (Now this man purchased a field with the wages of iniquity; and falling headlong, he burst open in the middle and all his entrails gushed out. And it became known to all those dwelling in Jerusalem; so that field is called in their own language, Akel Dama, that is, Field of Blood.) "For it is written in the book of Psalms: 'Let his dwelling place be desolate, And let no one live in it'; and, 'Let another take his office.'

"Therefore, of these men who have accompanied us all the time that the Lord Jesus went in and out among us, beginning from the baptism of John to that day when He was taken up from us, one of these must become a witness with us of His resurrection." And they proposed two: Joseph called Barsabas, who was surnamed Justus, and Matthias. And they prayed and said, "You, O Lord, who know the hearts of all, show which of these two You have chosen to take part in this ministry and apostleship from which Judas by transgression fell, that he might go to his own place." And they cast their lots, and the lot fell on Matthias. And he was numbered with the eleven apostles.

Acts 1:13-26

Some interpret the above scripture by finally saying that the selection of Matthias was a mistake on the part of Peter. The evidence for this statement is, "Matthias is never mentioned again anywhere in the Bible." While that statement is true, it is not evidence that Peter made an error by calling for the appointment of another disciple to take the place of Judas. The argument usually given is that God had already chosen Saul, who later became known as the apostle Paul, to be the replacement for Judas. Let us first look at the statement that you never find the name of Matthias after the first chapter of Acts, and see what we can learn from the list of apostles mentioned in the 13th verse shown below.

"Peter, James, John, and Andrew; Philip and Thomas; Bartholomew and Matthew; James the son of Alphaeus and Simon the Zealot; and Judas the son of James."

Let's see how many of them appear later in scripture.

1. **Peter** - Appears frequently in the early chapters of Acts. He preached the sermon that resulted in 3000 men plus women and children being added to the church on the day of Pentecost (Acts 2). God also used him to be the one who opened the way of salvation to the Gentiles (Acts 10). Peter was also at the conference held in the city of

Jerusalem to settle the issue of circumcision (Acts 15). He appears often in the beginning years of the church. Later, however, the book of Acts takes a turn and ends up speaking mostly about the ministry of Paul. Significantly, Peter wrote two epistles that bear his name. Obviously, Peter was a person of some importance and is mentioned quite often, even in Paul's first letter to the Corinthians, and his letter to the Galatians.

2. **James** - The son of Zebedee and brother of the apostle John. James was martyred by Herod in Jerusalem in Acts 12:1-2, otherwise, James is never mentioned after Acts 1:13.

3. **John** - The son of Zebedee and brother of the apostle James. John is mentioned in the early chapters of the book of Acts, but later, you read very little about him. John wrote a book containing a record of the acts of Jesus called *The Gospel According to John*. He also wrote three letters, and he finally ended up on the Isle of Patmos where he wrote the book of *Revelation* which is the last book in the New Testament.

4. **Andrew** - The brother of Peter is never mentioned after Acts 1:13.

5. **Philip** - Is never mentioned after Acts 1:13.

6. **Thomas** - Is never mentioned after Acts 1:13.

7. **Bartholomew** - Is never mentioned after Acts 1:13.

8. **Matthew** - Wrote *The Gospel According to Matthew*, but is never mentioned after Acts 1:13.

9. **James the son of Alphaeus** - Is never mentioned after Acts 1:13.

10. **Simon the zealot** - Is never mentioned after Acts 1:13.

11. **Judas the son of James** - Is never mentioned after Acts 1:13.

Of the eleven men mentioned as being apostles in the upper room, eight are never mentioned after Acts 1:13, Peter, James and John, who are mentioned were the three who were closest to Jesus during His earthly ministry. That Matthias was never mentioned after being appointed as an apostle puts him in some pretty good company, so to say the fact that you never read of Matthias after the first chapter of Acts proves that Peter made a mistake is just not borne out by scripture.

Who Was James?

The question naturally arises then, who was the apostle James you read about after James the brother of John was martyred in Acts 12, and who wrote the book of James. The apostle Paul can help us out with this.

> But when it pleased God, who separated me from my mother's womb and called me through His grace, to reveal His Son in me, that I might preach Him among the Gentiles, I did not immediately confer with flesh and blood, nor did I go up to Jerusalem to those who were apostles before me; but I went to Arabia, and returned again to Damascus. Then after three years I went up to Jerusalem to see Peter, and remained with him fifteen days. But I saw none of the other apostles except James, the Lord's brother.
> Galatians 1:15-19

In the first chapter of Galatians, when speaking of his conversion and training, Paul states that he "did not immediately confer with flesh an blood" showing that he did not want to be taught by men, so he "did not go up to . . . those who were apostles" before him. Instead, he went into the desert for a time. Then after three years he went to Jerusalem to see Peter for fifteen days. At that time, he did not see any of the other apostles except James, the brother of Jesus. Whenever you see James spoken of in the Bible after John's brother, James, was martyred in Acts 12, it is the Lord's brother who is referred to. Remember that during the earthly ministry of Jesus, His brother James was not a believer and he was not one of the original apostles.

> For even His brothers did not believe in Him.
> John 7:5

What About Philip?

Another question naturally arises regarding Philip the apostle. Someone named Philip is mentioned several times after Acts 1:13. Was this Philip the apostle?

We first read of this Philip in Acts 6:5 when he was appointed to be one of the seven deacons placed over the provision for the widows in the daily food distributions. When the need was brought to the attention of the apostles their reply was, "It is not desirable that we should leave the Word of God and serve tables." (Verse 2) This same Philip went to Samaria and preached the gospel as described in Acts 8:4-13. In verses 26-40 of the same chapter Philip was sent by the Holy Spirit to the road from Jerusalem to Gaza where he met the Ethiopian eunuch, whom he led to the Lord and baptized.

Finally in Acts 21:8 Luke calls this man "Philip the evangelist" saying, "On the next day we who were Paul's companions departed and came to Caesarea, and entered the house of Philip the evangelist, who was one of the seven, and stayed with him." This Philip was definitely not the apostle mentioned in Acts 1:13.

Two Different Commissions

Regarding the idea that God selected Paul to replace Judas, we need to understand that there were two different jobs given to the original apostles as compared to the job given to Paul. When Jesus sent His original selection of twelve on their first preaching and ministry journey he gave them a set of parameters for their task.

> These twelve Jesus sent out and commanded them, saying: **"Do not go into the way of the**

Gentiles, and do not enter a city of the Samaritans. But go rather to the **lost sheep of the house of Israel**."
Matthew 10:5-6 Emphasis added.

They were not to preach to Gentiles, but they were to seek out the "lost sheep of the *House of Israel*." Paul's commission was entirely different. Note what God told Ananias when he protested against visiting Paul after his conversion experience on the road to Damascus.

But the Lord said to him, "Go, for he is a chosen vessel of Mine **to bear My name before Gentiles, kings, and the children of Israel**."
Acts 9:15 Emphasis added.

The twelve were not sent to preach to Gentiles, but Paul's specific and primary calling was to reach Gentiles first of all, kings secondly, and finally "the children of Israel".
What did Peter say were the qualifications for one who would complete the group of twelve apostles?

"For it is written in the book of Psalms: 'Let his dwelling place be desolate, And let no one live in it'; and, 'Let another take his office.' "Therefore, of these men who **have accompanied us all the time that the Lord Jesus went in and out among us**, beginning from the baptism of John to that day when He was taken up from us, **one of these must become a witness with us of His resurrection**."
Acts 1:20-22 Emphasis added.

Peter listed the qualifications to be included with the remaining eleven apostles, namely that it must be someone who was with the original eleven from the preaching and baptism of

John, and who had been personally with Jesus during His earthly ministry. Why was that important? These twelve were then to be eye witnesses of the resurrection of Jesus. Paul could not speak of seeing the resurrected Jesus while He was still walking among the disciples. Paul himself makes an important statement in his chapter on the resurrection.

> For I delivered to you first of all that which I also received: that Christ died for our sins according to the Scriptures, and that He was buried, and that He rose again the third day according to the Scriptures, and that He was seen by Cephas, then **by the twelve.**
> I Corinthians 15:3-5 Emphasis added.

Paul clearly states that Jesus was seen after his resurrection "by the twelve." This could not have included Judas since Judas did not witness the resurrection, since he hanged himself when he knew that Jesus had been condemned.

> Then Judas, His betrayer, seeing that He had been condemned, was remorseful and brought back the thirty pieces of silver to the chief priests and elders, saying, "I have sinned by betraying innocent blood." And they said, "What is that to us? You see to it!" Then he threw down the pieces of silver in the temple and departed, and went and hanged himself.
> Matthew 27:3-5

The fact that Paul says Jesus was seen by "the twelve" means that he acknowledged Matthias as included in the number. Paul himself never thought he was a replacement for Judas.

The next question we need to address is, when Paul went to visit Peter around three years following his conversion, why didn't he see any of the twelve at Jerusalem except Peter and

James. The obvious answer is that they were not there! But where were they? The obvious answer is that they were seeking to complete the job Jesus gave to them.

> "But you shall receive power when the Holy Spirit
> has come upon you; and you shall be witnesses to
> Me in Jerusalem, and in all Judea and Samaria,
> and **to the end of the earth**."
> Acts 1:8 Emphasis added.

> These twelve Jesus sent out and commanded
> them, saying: "Do not go into the way of the
> Gentiles, and do not enter a city of the Samaritans.
> But go rather to **the lost sheep of the house of
> Israel**."
> Matthew 10:5-6 Emphasis added.

The majority of the apostles were going "to the end of the earth" in order to preach the gospel to the "lost sheep of the *House of Israel*," so naturally, they were not in Jerusalem when Paul arrived to visit Peter. The northern ten tribe *House of Israel* had been carried captive over seven hundred years earlier and were now settling into their new homes in northern Europe and the British Isles. While Paul spent most of his time preaching to Gentiles, "the twelve" were seeking for and having great success ministering to the non-Jewish, non-gentile *House of Israel*.

So, did Peter make a mistake in calling for the appointment of Matthias? The scriptural evidence says "No."

Appendix F

Similarities Between the Governmental Structures of the Anglo-Saxons and Ancient Israelites

The Founders of the United States, especially Thomas Jefferson, admired the institution of freedom under People's Law as practiced by the Anglo-Saxons. The main principal points of Anglo-Saxon People's Law (as described by Colin Rhys Lovell in *English Constitutional and Legal History*) are listed below:

- They considered themselves a commonwealth of freemen.
- All decisions and the selection of leaders had to be with the consent of the people, preferably by full consensus, not just a majority.
- The laws by which they were governed were considered natural laws given by divine dispensation, and were so well known by the people they did not have to be written down.
- Power was dispersed among the people and never allowed to concentrate in any one person or group. Even in time of war, the authority granted to the leaders was temporary and the power of the people to remove them was direct and simple.
- Primary responsibility for resolving problems rested first of all with the individual, then the family, then the tribe or community, then the region, and finally the nation.
- They were organized into small, manageable groups where every adult had a voice and a vote. They divided the people into units of ten families who elected a leader; then fifty families who elected a leader; then a hundred families who elected a leader; and then a thousand families who elected a leader.

- They believed the rights of the individual were considered unalienable and could not be violated without risking the wrath of divine justice as well as civil retribution by the people's judges.
- The system of justice was structured on the basis of severe punishment unless there was complete reparation to the person who had been wronged. There were only four "crimes" or offenses against the whole people. These were treason, by betraying their own people; cowardice, by refusing to fight or failing to fight courageously; desertion; and homosexuality. These were considered capital offenses. All other offenses required reparation to the person who had been wronged.
- They always attempted to solve problems on the level where the problem originated. If this was impossible they went no higher than was absolutely necessary to get a remedy. Usually only the most complex problems involving the welfare of the whole people, or a large segment of the people ever went to the leaders for solution.

As the Founders studied the record of ancient Israel they were intrigued by the fact that they also operated under a system of laws remarkably similar to those of the Anglo-Saxons. Here are the principal characteristics of the People's Law in ancient Israel which were almost identical with those of the Anglo-Saxons.

- They were set up as a commonwealth of freemen. A basic tenet was: "Proclaim liberty throughout all the land unto all the inhabitants thereof." (Leviticus 25:10)
- All the people were organized into small manageable units where the representative of each family had a voice and a vote. This organizing process was launched after Jethro, the father-in-law of Moses, saw him trying to govern the people under Ruler's Law. (See Exodus 18:13-

26) When the structure was completed Israel was organized like this:

Moses

Internal Affairs - **Aaron – Joshua** - Military Leader

Council of Seventy

Elected Representatives

*600 Groups of   1,000 Families

*6,000 Groups of   100   Families

*12,000 Groups of   50   Families

*60,000 Groups of   10   Families

More than 600 Thousand Families
More than 3 Million People with Power
To Govern Themselves

*These numbers are estimations based on the census
recorded
in the first chapter of the book of Numbers

- There was specific emphasis on strong, local self-government. Problems were solved to the greatest possible extent on the level where they originated. The record says: "The hard cases they brought to Moses, but they judged every small case themselves." (Exodus 18:26)
- The entire code of justice was based primarily on reparation to the victim rather than fines and punishment by the commonwealth. (See Exodus chapters 21 and 22) The one crime for which no "satisfaction" could be given

was first-degree murder. The penalty was death. (See Numbers 35:31)

- Leaders were elected and new laws were approved by the common consent of the people. (See II Samuel 2:4, I Chronicles 29:22; for the rejection of a leader, see II Chronicles 10:16; for the approval of new laws, see Exodus 19:8)
- Accused persons were presumed to be innocent until proven guilty. Evidence had to be strong enough to remove any question of doubt as to guilt. Borderline cases were decided in favor of the accused and he was released. It was felt that if he were actually guilty, his punishment could be left to the judgement of God in the future life.

The preceding information was taken from *The 5000 Year Leap* by W. Cleon Skousen pages 12 - 17.

Bibliography

Judah's Sceptre and Joseph's Birthright - J. H. Allen - Destiny Publishers Merrimac , MA www.destinypublishers.com

The United States and Britain in Prophecy - Herbert W. Armstrong - published by Philadelphia Church of God 1945 and 2007 editions.

Jeremiah in Ireland - John E. Wall - http://www.ensignmessage.com/archives/jeremiahinireland.html (accessed March 12, 2010)

Scotland's Stone of Destiny - Nick Aitchison - Tempus Publishing, Ltd, The Mill, Brimscombe Port, Stroud, Gloucestershire GL5 2QG

The Great Seal of the United States - Author Unknown

NOVUS ORDO SECLORUM – Origin and Meaning of the Motto Beneath the American Pyramid - Author Unknown - www.greatseal.com/mottoes/seclorum.html (accessed March 12, 2010)

The Royal House of Britain An Enduring Dynasty - The Rev. W. M. H. Milner M.A. - The Covenant Publishing Co., Ltd., London

Adam Clark's Commentary - Adam Clark - WORDsearch bible software Database © 2004 - WORDsearch Corporation

Jamieson-Fausset-Brown Bible Commentary - Electronic text and markup copyright 1999 by Epiphany Software.

Israel Ministry of Foreign Affairs Web Site - Balfour Declaration Page -

http://www.mfa.gov.il/MFA/Peace+Process/Guide+to+the+Peace+Process/The+Balfour+Declaration.htm (accessed March 12, 2010)

"I Have Loved Jacob" - Dr. Joseph Hoffman Cohn - American Board of Missions to the Jews, Inc, Orangeburg, N.Y.

The Lineal Descent of the Royal Family of England - http://www.libraryireland.com/Pedigrees1/RoyalFamilyEngland.php (accessed March 12, 2010)

The Brit-Am Web Site - http://www.britam.org/ (accessed March 12, 2010)

The 5000 Year Leap - W. Cleon Skousen - National Center for Constitutional Studies - www.nccs.net (accessed March 12, 2010)

To Contact the Author

Email: info@michaeldhodge.com

Web Site: www.michaeldhodge.com

Made in the USA
Charleston, SC
18 June 2011